Forum's Principles of Learning:

A Guidebook for Advancing Performance in Today's Workplace

Forum

Contents

Preface

Preface

Executives at a manufacturing company acknowledged they had a "people pipeline problem." They were grappling with two major workforce issues: How would the company be impacted when a significant number of employees retired and took their know-how with them? And how could the firm address the needs of younger, tech-savvy workers transitioning into senior management ranks while sufficiently advancing the corporate mission and improving its strategic speed?

These are mission-critical issues and are challenges that executives are confronting on a global level, as we at The Forum Corporation learned from the senior-level interviews and research we recently conducted.

At the manufacturing company mentioned above, the Learning and Development group was charged with figuring out the course of action. Its first steps involved establishing a comprehensive, community-centric program for the next generation of leaders in the organization. Over 18 months, community members attended classes, participated in expert roundtable luncheon discussions, and worked through business problems together. They moved through the program as a group, but also created a space where individual competency development and concerns about their unique needs were shared. Participants were encouraged to seek out organization experts—regardless of age or corporate rank—and use threaded discussions and ongoing communities of practice to solve business issues. In addition, participants documented their learning in a program blog.

This type of layered, continuous learning environment opened up several opportunities for the manufacturing company. Primarily, it helped executives avoid the leadership vacuum they anticipated would exist when senior managers retired and younger workers stepped into their positions. It also engaged teams in a collaborative, cross-generational, skills-swapping dialog and leveraged various community-building tools aimed at improving the groups' learning goals. As a result of the program, a significant number of promotions were credited to the relationships formed during the course of the program.

Companies—and more specifically, their Learning and Development (L&D) groups—are confronted with challenges like this more and more every day. The workplace, already a multi-faceted web of complexity, demands innovative, learning-centric management solutions as the face of the global workforce continues to change. While researching this report, we observed some common patterns emerging among leading companies addressing these issues, and we will provide those insights here.

We will also answer two pressing questions weighing on many executives' minds: How exactly does the L&D industry leap into this brave new world? And how can it better prepare itself for these inevitable workforce shifts while, at the same time, keeping the company moving forward in quick time toward its business objectives? This report provides guidance by building on tried-and-true business wisdom Forum has acquired over the years and by challenging companies to go even further in embracing cutting-edge tools, practices, and learning concepts.

Executive Overview

Executive Overview

Most companies today are looking to go faster, be more responsive to customer demands, and grab greater market share with groundbreaking products and services. But, even as they stare these dilemmas down and do their best to achieve these goals, a number of factors hold companies back from realizing the full potential of their mission-critical initiatives.

"The future of organizations today is primarily related to their capacity to learn."

George Siemens, Technology Enhanced Knowledge Research Institute (TEKRI), Athabasca University

We're not only referring to the traditional, well-known obstacles most companies already have to manage—things like globalized operations, economic uncertainty, strategic speed bumps, and information overload. We're seeing four other trends weaving their way into boardroom conversations, goading executives to rethink their strategic and tactical business plans, and pressure-testing longstanding workplace learning methods. Let's take a closer look at these latest issues demanding Learning and Development ingenuity.

- **Bringing learning closer to the work.** To increase organizational speed and effectively cultivate experience, that is, to learn and improve from experience continuously, corporate learning efforts must be closely integrated with the work at hand. In the recent past, many organizations separated learning from the work by focusing primarily on event-based learning programs. Often held off-site and lasting upwards of 2 days, these sessions were designed to create a targeted learning experience away from the daily work. As organizations cope with a changing workforce, globalization, and economic pressures, there is a growing desire to directly integrate learning experiences into the flow and context of daily work. Said simply, the learning is now the work and the work is the learning.

- **Making sense of the growing number of available learning tools.** New tools affect the "who, when, and where" of workplace learning. However, the rapid evolution of Web-based tools, the growing ubiquity of smart, mobile devices, and increased connectivity requirements have all impacted the way organizations function. Successful companies figure how to leverage the ones that make sense for their learning communities.

- **Becoming cultivators of learning.** L&D's role continues to be in transition, moving from a primary focus on developing learning curriculums to an expanded role as cultivators of learning. Based on our discussions with learning thought leaders and clients, along with our growing body of research, it is clear that L&D must manage the corporate culture in a way that captures everyday learning and creates a rich database of experienced-based knowledge. This is a leadership practice that will differentiate organizations today and in the future.

- **Managing new leaders and new workplace dynamics.** Many companies are beginning to see what happens when next-generation workers move into management positions. Because younger workers come with different skills and expectations, this generational shift is changing how many companies work and learn. It also puts pressure on L&D executives to creatively develop tools that appeal to all employees while appropriately addressing evolving learning behaviors and work patterns.

This last point is worth paying particularly close attention to, especially as more companies—like the manufacturing firm we used as an example in the Preface—see their workforce dynamics shift in the wake of millennials entering management ranks. We use the term "millennial" intentionally loosely to indicate a range of younger workers now entering the management workforce, without earmarking a specific group based on their birth year. Of course, all generations have their quirks, and generalizations like this cannot account for individual differences and exceptions. Also, depending on where you are on the globe, your perspective on generational trends, and their accuracy in characterizing the experiences and behaviors of you and your cultural peers, might be quite different.

But, there is one thing for certain: This next generation worker has grown up in a highly connected world and has been strongly influenced by technology. That twist in life experience exerts a discernable impact on workplace learning for all of us, and it is this impact that we feel compelled to explore.

In this report, we examine these evolutionary trends through the lens of traditional workplace learning principles, in-depth research findings, illustrative case examples, and strategic calls-to-action.

Section 1:
About the Research

About the Research

Emerging trends in the business world have been the impetus for The Forum Corporation to recently examine its own body of research, spark additional thought-provoking discussions about the shifting business climate, and assess sweet spots where L&D professionals can and should invest time, energy, and resources. Our recent research on strategic speed found that companies that take time to "cultivate experience" are better able to execute strategy with speed—so with this project we are taking our own medicine.

"The irony is that nonstop action leads to zero cultivation of experience and, in the end, less speed."

Jocelyn Davis, et al., The Forum Corporation, Strategic Speed: Mobilize People, Accelerate Execution

Forum's original research on the topic of workplace learning was published in 1978 by several authors, including George Litwin, under the title "Principles of Adult Learning." This seminal work was updated by Joan Bragar and Kerry Johnson in 1993. Building on that solid base, Tom Atkinson and Jocelyn Davis published the foundational "Principles of Workplace Learning" in 2003. As we reflected on that work through the mirror of today's most urgent challenges, we found that our six foundational principles remain mission-critical L&D levers for any business struggling to make heads or tails of the current learning climate. They are ground rules that can be built upon as business scenarios shift. They are:

1. Link Learning to Value for the Individual and the Organization

2. Connect Action and Reflection in a Continuous Cycle

3. Address Learners' Attitudes and Beliefs in Addition to Their Behaviors

4. Provide Learners with a Balance of Challenge and Support

5. Create Opportunities for Participants to Teach as Well as Learn

6. Design and Cultivate Learning Communities Along with Learning Media

The goal of this research project was to test, revalidate, and refine these principles as they apply to the current business environment.

THE METHODS

In addition to drawing on our recent research findings, for this report we also interviewed over 60 experts, in fields such as neuroscience, learning and development, psychology, and learning technology. These experts are thought leaders in their areas of expertise, with an average experience of 20 years; their knowledge spans a broad range of companies and industries around the world. A description of these contributors is provided in the Acknowledgments section. We also conducted a thorough review of the workplace learning literature (see Bibliography).

THE OUTPUTS

The research has yielded two main outputs:

- **An expanded set of principles to guide the development of workplace learning.** These principles can serve as guideposts for designing workplace learning, and, if followed closely, will accelerate the cultivation of experience.

- **A process for making decisions about the development and deployment of learning solutions in today's organization.** These tools provide guidance in selecting, sequencing, and applying learning methods that will help organizations cultivate experience through complete learning solutions.

We hope that leaders will find the strategies in this report helpful, as they strive to create organizations that compete and win in the workplace of tomorrow.

Section 2:
The Principles

Principle 1:

Link Learning to Value for the Individual and the Organization

Principle 1: Link Learning to Value for the Individual and the Organization

Learning and Development teams frequently find themselves between a rock and a hard place. On one side, top management relies on the L&D group to help transform high-level business obstacles into financial and operational performance improvements. Not surprisingly, many senior managerial focus areas today tend to revolve around the need for strategic speed, a key concern vocalized by leaders interviewed in our recent Global Speed Survey. About 90 percent of the 343 respondents agreed that speed in strategic execution was critical to their business. However, many respondents also acknowledged that there were sizeable gaps when it came to actually being able to execute, assess, and correct strategic plans in a fully efficient manner—which then affected their overall perception of speediness. Additionally, other industry studies show that leaders view "responsiveness to changes in the environment" and "swift adaptability to change" as critical competitive advantages and the greatest management challenge in the future.[1] With these challenges in mind, organizations want their L&D teams to appropriately match learning initiatives with the anticipated organizational value generated when companies move faster and hit desired business milestones.

In addition to that organizational value, L&D has another set of concerns when working on the individual level. Individuals value workplace learning differently than organizations do. They want their learning customized to the challenge at hand, delivered when they need it, and intimately connected to advancing their careers. This becomes even more pressing as a new generation of workers transitions to management roles. Today's new generation, which we refer to as "millennials," has been raised on a steady diet of readily available online access to learning assets, and are adept at finding whatever information they need with a few keyboard strokes. However, they don't just see the online world as a resource to mine, they are active participants. They are writers, producers, bloggers, and videographers who are incredibly comfortable with contributing and discussing information with online communities.

The tension between the organizational and individual learning needs presents a dilemma for L&D: How can the group balance these sometimes-conflicting needs and find ways to connect value to learning for both constituents?

> "The learning must be contextual, a way for individuals to see their work in relationship to the whole organization."
>
> *George Siemens, Technology Enhanced Knowledge Research Institute (TEKRI) at Athabasca University*

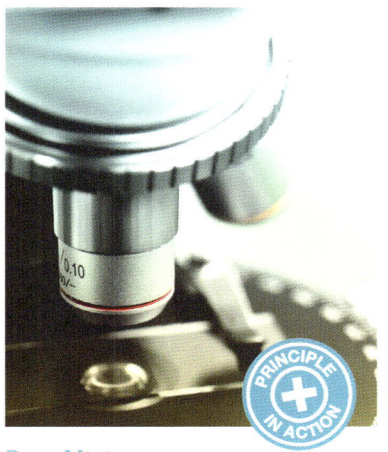

Data Mining & Analytics

A new manager is working on a contract for a major oil manufacturer. He is based in Europe, but his counterparts are in the U.S. and South America. As he begins to send e-mails, create documents, and request data, the supporting technology is able to recognize the pattern of his work and the way the information flows.

The underlying analytic technology helps the manager creatively identify other patterns and projects that might serve as a model to other teams. Connecting with those teams, in turn, provides the opportunity to share expertise that could add value to his project. In this case, the technology and related learning mechanisms serve as a "sense-making system," supporting what the manager is trying to accomplish and ultimately enabling collaboration across the entire enterprise.

We know there is a shift happening: Most organizations are experiencing a moderate volume of younger workers entering their organization and, as the boomer generation retires, we expect this figure to rise. These younger workers bring new expectations for how they learn and interact. In a 2009 study conducted by Bersin & Associates of more than 40,000 training, HR, and business leaders around the world, 40 percent of respondents stated that their challenge in training younger workers is "very large or significant."[2]

There is intense focus on projecting how this younger group of workers will impact organizations, and the answer often boils down to: "It depends." It depends on how large this group is in your organization, the strength of your corporate culture, and the cultural demographics of your workforce. What we do know is that the rising generational influence will change how we work and learn. According to the Bersin study, 77 percent of respondents believe that the learning needs of these younger workers are different than those of the rest of the workforce.

To advance our understanding of this millennial group, we dug a little deeper to understand how millennials prefer to learn. The research available highlights these emerging learning preferences:[3]

- Communal learning that involves diverse, tacit, immersed experience, and generates knowledge that is distributed across the community

- A balance among experiential learning, guided mentoring, and collective reflection

- Expression through nonlinear, associational webs of representations

- Co-design of learning experiences personalized to individual needs and preferences

Today's workers value connection and context, and they have the tools and skills to create both if they are not provided by the organizations they work for. This sometimes leads to a perception that they are disloyal and/or disrespectful because they may break organizational norms in pursuit of satisfying their own learning needs. Generally the perception of millennial disloyalty is mostly unfounded. Based on our understanding of the research, millennials may demonstrate skepticism about corporate mandates, but they also tend to be strong advocates for their own group's success and frequently take initiative to advance their own and their team's capabilities.

New 360–Degree Assessment

A major energy company switched things up by designing and deploying a new 360-degree assessment leadership development system. To make such a comprehensive task less onerous for the individual to complete and the corporation to manage and analyze, the assessment model required the participating top organizational leaders to identify—via a new multi-rater feedback survey—only their top three personal strengths and areas for development. The resultant limited, bite-sized chunks of data helped focus development direction for the individual as well as improve the efficiency and effectiveness of the manager's coaching feedback processes.

At the same time, organizations are placing an increased value on workers with tacit skills—workers who must exchange information, make judgments, and collaborate with others in order to do their jobs. The development of these skills has become a dominant theme for L&D professionals around the world. Between 25 and 50 percent of today's workforce has jobs that are primarily focused on tacit activities, according to industry reports.[4] In industries with a preponderance of tacit interactions like sales, marketing, engineering, and financial services, companies that understood how to increase the effectiveness of these tacit workers showed a significant performance lead over those in the same industry who focused primarily on improving efficiency.[5]

The good news is that as individuals increasingly value connection and context, so do organizations. The emerging challenge for L&D is providing learning in a way that is very individualized, links the individual to the work and to others doing similar work, and builds a collective pool of knowledge that the organization can leverage to bring value to the business. In response to this challenge, L&D experts are moving from facilitators of learning to curators and cultivators of a learning ecosystem. They are being asked to enable knowledge sharing and access; to distribute expertise; to sieve, synthesize, and catalog valuable learning experiences; and to look for opportunities to make sense of the wealth of institutional knowledge in their organization. To be effective in this new role and to create value both on the individual and organizational level, they must create, seek out, and pull together various sources of knowledge, ensure that learning is captured, and measure the effectiveness and the results for the organization.

STRATEGIES

As the balance of L&D responsibility shifts away from curriculum development to the creation and management of disaggregated chunks of learning, there is a corresponding shift in the L&D professional's day-to-day role. Accomplishing these tasks involves adopting a variety of strategies, which we see as:

- Break learning down into smaller pieces
- Use technology to support the learning ecosystem
- Cultivate learning communities
- Expand learning methods

Modern Mentoring

Sometimes the right tool at the right time is just the trick to bring value to learning for the individual and the corporation. A large mortgage company sought to promote informal learning and mentorship. They also hoped to introduce social learning technology tools in a way that would have meaning to the organization and align with its corporate objectives. Combining the two goals, the company created an automated process to pair mentors and protégées. The system included directed use of social learning tools to support, and, over time, invigorate the mentoring relationships. The system's assessment metrics, comparing results to established individual and company goals, ensured the value of learning was brought home for both parties.

Break Learning Down into Smaller Pieces

In response to these influences, many organizations are adopting an approach that puts smaller work learning assets, tailored to support specific individuals or situations, right into the flow of the work. These "disaggregated," customized chunks of learning often live online and work well for both the individual and the organization. Interestingly, this approach also seems to work well for older generations, no doubt due to the convenience and easy access.

Use Technology to Support the Learning Ecosystem

Web 2.0 and social networking tools can help filter and harness the fire-hose flow of information and data coming at us on a daily basis. What's more, these tools can be used to capture and share experiences and knowledge within the organization. Ten years ago, we did not record most of the work done in an organization on a day-to-day basis. Today, by contrast, we automatically capture most of our daily work. It's there—in our e-mails, our electronic documents, our postings and recordings—tucked into the nooks and crannies of an organization. L&D can use these new tools to connect the dots.

Successful companies have long deemed critical the investment in organizational knowledge structures, social networking tools, and analytics. These powerful tools make it possible to track information exchanges, efficiently connect employees with needed knowledge, mine team and community correspondence and documents for valuable lessons, determine the validity of information based on social connections, and leverage the existing expertise in the organization. Ultimately, they help link value to the organization and its individual contributors by meeting both of their needs.

Cultivate Learning Communities

Social learning networks, or communities of practice, have increasingly become a preferred platform to connect a dynamic array of people and information brought together for the express purpose of supporting individual and group learning as well as a specific task or project. Not surprisingly, these networks have great appeal to the new generation of workers, not only because this is how they often interact outside of work, but also because millennials tend to have a greater loyalty to a local team or community than they do to the corporation as a whole.

Learning communities (which we'll examine again in Principle 6) flourish because they successfully address the value proposition for both the individual and the organization. By playing up the value of the local, smaller community, the individual prospers and grows because his or her immediate and unique learning needs are met in a timely fashion. Similarly, the specialized knowledge and learning that can be found *in* the network can be extracted and later shared across the organization, thus increasing learning's value to the entire company and providing a repository of readily accessible useful information. Also, the organization reaps the benefits of greater productivity that comes from increasingly efficient, individualized learning successes.

Expand Learning Methods

Job rotations, targeted work assignments, and mentoring are tried and tested ways for organizations to respond to the specific needs of the business. Historically deployed to a select group of "fast track" executives, these methods offer some of the best opportunities to link individual and organizational value. One specific approach is to provide training and short-term job trials in other functional areas within the organization. This approach creates opportunities for employees to pursue on-the-job challenges and diversify their skills while raising their visibility in the organization. The organization gains increased cross-functional awareness and unity through understanding, and increases the bench strength of individuals with varied experience and skills. Technology tools help overcome the barrier of distance and allow the approach to be cost-effectively deployed to many workers, not just to senior managers.

Principle 2:
Connect Action and Reflection in a Continuous Cycle

Principle 2: Connect Action and Reflection in a Continuous Cycle

Today's information explosion and fast-paced, competitive business environment compels us to act and to act *now*. Consequently, we increasingly and appropriately require workplace learning to be immediate, relevant, and more highly applicable to the overall business goals than ever before. Naturally, we shortchange reflection in favor of action.

"The faster the pace, the more reflection is needed."

Judy Francolini, Executive Coach, Forum Associate

However, reflection, or sense making, is the adhesive that makes learning stick—without it, learning leaves no mark and slips away. Behavior change and course-correcting activities will not happen if people have no insight into their actions or a way to make sense of them. Reflection creates psychological distance from the work, which allows people to examine experiences, find meaning in them, generate new knowledge, and change behavior. These reflective actions, as we discovered during our research, tend to have a positive impact on corporate productivity, strategic speed, and business results. In fact, our Global Speed Survey revealed that faster companies often had adopted structures that supported the concept of "slowing down to move faster"; speediness, at these companies, resulted when business leaders encouraged teams to take time and review the work being done.

It's easy to say, "take a moment," but, really, how does reflection actually work? How can L&D encourage senior management and the workforce to take time to reflect in an environment of extreme constraints and immense pressure to act quickly?

RESEARCH FINDINGS

Our research confirms the wisdom of Socrates and, later, John Dewey and Daniel Schon (and most likely, all L&D professionals): Successful learning must consist of action—mental, physical, or both—in conjunction with an opportunity to reflect on, or process, the action and its outcome. People learn by doing and by then thinking about what they have done. The iterative action-reflection-action-reflection cycle generates retention and direction for future action and allows people to examine experiences, find meaning in them, and generate new insight and knowledge. This action and reflection cycle stokes the learning engine, allowing us to learn and improve from experience continuously—that is, to cultivate and harvest our own experiences—and thus improve productivity and business results.

To better understand the importance of reflection as it relates to an individual's ability to learn, it's useful to briefly examine the way it works in our brains. Research from the neurosciences makes clear that when we reflect, we process, record, retain, and add more information to a memory. Reflecting creates associations and improves what brain researchers call "lateral thinking." Lateral thinking refers to an indirect reasoning method

Stop & Think

A representative from a large energy company explains that the rate of change and the volume of work are used as convenient excuses to forgo necessary reflection. No one ever thinks they have the time to stop and think.

To address this issue, the L&D professionals have begun to actively provide managers with guidance on how to help employees make reflection a part of their work. Some techniques include providing managers with a project debrief process, encouraging the use of inquiry as a management technique, and reinforcing the important role managers play by setting the example for reflection. In addition to developing managers as leaders of a reflective culture, all training conducted by the L&D team includes structured reflection, demonstrating reflections effectiveness as a tool for learning.

where new ideas are obtained via tangential or non-obvious pathways. During this process of recall and focus (thinking about it), your conscious attention makes senses of the new information, connects it with other knowledge you possess, and increases your retention and comprehension. This, then, triggers a series of other responses from the brain, which also sparks an emotional reaction to the information being processed. In light of this process, action and reflection must be well connected in order to yield techniques and strategies that produce results for the learner and the organization. Additionally, learners must take appropriate next steps based on those reflections.

There is also an emotional context in which the reflection process occurs and impacts our effectiveness. Along these lines, we find that when a person is challenged that challenge has a positive effect on the person's ability to focus. However, in highly stressful situations, stress hormones create a threat response in the brain region know as the amygdala (or emotional reaction center). This physiological response overwhelms rational thinking and interrupts smooth functioning of the executive and decision-making regions of the brain. Therefore, your thinking and your reflections will not be as productive if conducted under stress. So, workplace climate is critical: If people feel threatened or fearful, they will not be able to reflect, or learn, effectively.

But when is the right time to reflect? Most organizations think formal reflection typically comes after an event, but Ron Heifetz, in his book *The Practice of Adaptive Leadership,* makes an interesting point on reflecting in the midst of action—what Heifetz calls "moving off the dance floor" and "getting on the balcony." It's a way to gain perspective and observe yourself and others in order to detect and interpret patterns. When we reflect while we work, and when we connect our action and reflection as a daily practice, we can increase the quality and the speed of our learning and, by default, our work. This continuous and embedded cycle of action and reflection accurately reflects the way successful work and learning are increasingly intertwined.

So far we have examined these ideas from the perspective of the individual—how individuals think and reflect. While taking stock in isolation is an essential skill, our research—and our experience—tells us that we can also achieve productive outcomes when we reflect with others. Although there is a subjective element to reflection, there is a relational aspect to it as well. Learning, as we know, is often social. In a world of information abundance, our best solutions come from connecting and sense-making with others—within and amongst teams, between and among those who have and share data, and with customers.

Live-blog the Event.

Due to budget cuts only one person on the engineering team at a major technology company could attend the industry's national conference in Indianapolis. A creative member of the L&D group turned what might have been a morale problem into an intriguing opportunity to practice reflection in action. When the engineering team's representative was told she would be able to go the conference, the L&D professional suggested that she live blog the conference. To get up to speed on blogging, the engineer spent time reviewing other blogs and sharing notes with colleagues who frequently blogged.

After each conference session, she posted a brief description, noting emerging trends, providing links to cited papers, and capturing the dominant take-home messages. Back in the office, her colleagues read her posts as they went up and replied in the comments sections. Other team members asked her questions, requested clarifications, and made suggestions about other sessions to attend or people to meet. As a result, everyone on the team had a presence at the meeting and the company's representative had the opportunity to reflect in action while processing the conference information and forming a deeper understanding of what she learned.

In much the same way that we know that learning is often social, connected reflection with others also serves as a catalyst for change—a change of knowledge, a change of awareness, and, more importantly, a change in behavior. (The behavioral aspects of learning will be examined in Principle 5.)

Organizationally, L&D must address the challenge of creating time and space for adequate reflection on the individual and enterprise levels. We offer these strategies to help L&D teams move in this direction:

- Engineer learning experiences on the job

- Include reflection in coaching conversations

- Make reflection part of the work

- Diversify the learning tool kit to encourage reflection

Engineer Learning Experiences on the Job

On-the-job learning experiences are particularly beneficial, and managers should take advantage of them and engineer them thoughtfully. These are rich experiences that serve as springboards to future action and, possibly, best corporate practices. Projects that demand new and different capabilities— for example, stepping into another employee's role or regular job rotation—can further lead to additional understanding and experience. To make the most of these experiences, L&D professionals should encourage people to be conscious of their actions, aware of their reflection activity, and diligent in sharing their learning with the rest of the organization. By including reflection in these routine experiences, employees will process and identify opportunities for improvement, and better retain what they've learned. Similarly, their learning will be more intentional and closer to the work, which fosters increased efficiency, effectiveness, and speedier strategic execution.

Include Reflection in Coaching Conversations

L&D professionals don't need to be convinced about the value of coaching—they know it works. However, many of the experts we interviewed stress the importance of adding the element of reflection to coaching sessions. David Rock, author and coach, suggests his own ARIA model as a way to do this, with ARIA meaning Awareness, Reflection, Insight, and Action. Awareness is a reminder to stop and focus on a particular challenge or one part of a problem. Coaches encourage reflection by asking questions that cause people to give more attention to the problem and

Reflection-on-Action in Mentoring

A Canadian university's peer-to-peer student tutoring program employs reflection-on-action to improve mentor instruction and support. All peer mentors receive basic training before engaging in tutoring. In addition, some peer mentors receive ongoing feedback and support through an online journal system, which records communications between peer mentors and their university supervisors. The journals serve at least three reflection-on-action purposes: They are an instructive transcript of the interaction between a given peer mentor and supervisor pairing; they provide record of an individual peer mentor's competency development, and they are a rich data source for conducting in-depth comparative analysis and identifying program commonalities and trends. Such structured reflection ensures thoughtful peer mentor improvement as well as refined and increasingly effective program training materials, instruction, and support.

quietly reflect on possible solutions. *Insights,* coming from the coached worker, should be nurtured via another question-answer round that goes beyond the initial reflection. A good coach then motivates the worker to take *action* quickly on the heels of an insight. By using a model like this, coaches can help employees build self-observation and reflection into their daily activities and improve their overall learning capabilities.

Make Reflection Part of the Work

It can be extremely challenging to maintain a discipline of intentional reflection. While reflection activities encourage people to pause, evaluate, and become aware of their new knowledge, they are most useful when practiced on a regular basis, as part of daily work. In this way, reflection can move from occurring *on* action to be used more strategically *in* action.

The U.S. Army's practice of after-action reviews (AARs) is a well-known example of reflection in action and how it can be integrated into the daily workflow. Developed by the United States Army's National Training Center more than 25 years ago, AARs—conducted as sit-downs in the field or in the offices of battalion leaders—are a reflective planning method used to extract lessons from one event or project and apply them to another. On the face of it, AAR is a simple practice deployed throughout the chain of command. Each AAR sets out to answer four questions:

- What did we set out to do?
- What happened?
- Why did it happen?
- What are we going to do about it?

The iterations of the practice quickly build on each other and sum to what the Army calls a "vertical impact."

A 2005 Harvard Business Review article, "Learning in the Thick of It" brought this armed forces technique into wider acceptance in the business world.[6] In their work, Darling et al. draw an important distinction between the military's AAR practice and the more typically encountered retrospectives performed by many businesses, where learning happens at the end of a project. Effective AAR meetings, conducted by small, task-focused groups, center on key issues related to progress, and take place through the life of a project. In recent years, companies like Shell Oil, Harley-Davidson, and IBM have all demonstrated success with the technique.

Diversify the Learning Tool Kit to Encourage Reflection

Reflection can, and does, take place in any number of ways, and L&D professionals should remain open-minded when it comes to tools used to encourage and capture reflective experiences and actions.

Christian Briggs, Instructor in New Media Theory at Indiana University School of Informatics, points out that people who are savvy with new media tools (such as blogging and other social media) often use them for reflection in action. These tools allow people to record and share their reflections, add them to the collective wisdom, and spark ongoing conversations that deepen the experience. As Briggs describes it, a satisfying, self-perpetuating, continuous cycle emerges as the very same tools help the people who use them become more reflective in their work.

For starters, L&D can contribute blog posts and comments on a company-wide blog on issues related to business, workplace learning, and performance. Modeling reflection and conversation using social media like this invites participation from others in a way that can increase reflection, bootstrap learning, connect learners, and reinforce learning throughout the organization. Companies can build from there as workers become more comfortable engaging in that kind of environment.

Another approach comes out of the manufacturing sector's model of rapid prototyping, which actively links the action-reflection cycle. Rather than sink significant money and time into full-fledged product development, nimble organizations first put together a prototype, test it with customers, assess the results, revamp, and repeat. While "reflection" is sometimes mistakenly equated with "slowness," incorporating such reflection into the development cycle actually increases the speed (and quality) of R&D by efficiently assessing trials and ultimately reducing the number of failures in the field.

The prototyping approach can, of course, be applied to all sorts of jobs and situations. Managers can promote learning by encouraging their employees to get a task or output "roughly right," test it or gather feedback, reflect on the results, revise it, and try again. As David Kelley, chief executive officer of IDEO Product Development (one of the most successful product design consulting firms in the world) likes to say, "Enlightened trial and error outperforms the planning of flawless intellects."[7]

Principle 3:

Address Learners' Attitudes and Beliefs in Addition to Their Behaviors

Principle 3: Address Learners' Attitudes and Beliefs in Addition to Their Behaviors

OVERVIEW

To understand whether someone learned something, you would monitor his or her behaviors, right? You can actually assess learning in this way—to a degree. However, to know whether a person truly internalized something, you have to look deeper, measuring changes to the attitudes and beliefs, often referred to as "mental models." Think of a mental model as a model of the way the world works, a sort of shortcut that allows us to quickly process the massive information overflow that we encounter every day.

Mental models drive behaviors long term. That is because people's view of themselves and of their world—their beliefs, attitudes, and feelings about what happens to them and how they should respond—deeply affects learning, and the behaviors they keep or change.

In fact, almost 60 years ago, learning theorist Jean Piaget showed that for learning to last, mental models must be identified, evaluated, tested, and—in some cases—challenged. This is the type of learning that allows someone to revise or create new mental models and operate in new ways.

RESEARCH FINDINGS

As mentioned in Principle 2 we know from decades of work in the field of cognitive psychology (recently corroborated by research in neuroscience) that the first step in learning is to transfer information from short to long-term memory. This transfer takes place best when the new information can be connected to existing knowledge, a process Piaget called "assimilation." But what happens when you assimilate knowledge that doesn't really reflect an accurate or appropriate mental model? If the knowledge is misconceived, inaccurate, outdated, or biased, then assimilating new information will only perpetuate inappropriate attitudes, unfounded beliefs, and unacceptable behaviors.

Sometimes the mental model must change (a process Piaget referred to as "accommodation") in order for a person to be more effective in the world. For example, leaders must sometimes shed old mental models about leadership ("leaders must have the answer") and acclimate to new information and ways of working ("the most effective leaders coach and collaborate rather than tell"). There are myriad influences on an individual's mental models. Here we focus on the four most powerful influences operating in today's workplace. Being aware of and understanding how these influences shape attitudes and beliefs will help L&D design the type of effective and lasting learning experiences that shift mental models and the behaviors they drive.

Four Generations

An L&D professional at a major energy company explains that four generations of workers are employed at the company. The range of needs in the various populations and the tools that have had to be deployed to meet these needs has surprised her.

In her day-to-day work, she explains, it's critical to understand and address pre-existing attitudes and beliefs when designing learning solutions. For example, a large portion of the firm's population is comprised of nuclear engineers who began their career in the military where chain of command is part of the culture. When creating learning solutions for this segment of the organization, the L&D professional tries to broaden the learners' collaborative and decision-making experiences beyond the hierarchical mental models they may be predisposed to.

Generational Differences Affect Mental Models

In the U.S. in particular, we are starting to see some key distinctions among the younger and older generations' attitudes, beliefs, and expectations. While these differences may not yet be so obvious in other regions, in many developing countries, the younger generation far outnumbers the older one. Therefore, it's critical for leaders of multinational or global companies to understand how these age differences affect employees, and how work-related expectations and behaviors take shape.

Generational experts note these key differences in the learning preferences of this generation:

- Millennials are more fluent with new media and spend more time using online tools for communication.

- Many younger workers prefer electronic communication to face-to-face dialog, particularly when it comes to content that is emotional or confrontational in nature.

- Millennials need reward and recognition, but are not necessarily focused on financial gains.

- They report less loyalty to the organization and more loyalty to the team and the local community.

These differences naturally affect the mental models of younger managers entering the organization, rendering a different attitude toward work. The best organizational response, of course, is to treat any generational differences just as you would any other diversity issue (such as cultural, ethnic, or geographical) in the workplace—with respectful curiosity, compassion, and compromise.

Technology Affects Mental Models

The ever-evolving nature of technology means that employees must constantly adapt and adjust. More importantly, it means that employees enter the workplace with different mental models about the purpose, usefulness, and value of technology for work.

L&D is increasingly important in a technology-rich and enabled age when executives mandate that learning and business functions be tightly integrated to enhance the acquisition of skills and increased productivity. Moreover, many companies have created technology-based workplace learning, which requires workers to have a certain technical sophistication in order to leverage learning and development systems, find the information they need, and communicate effectively with their peers.

**Make Learning
Intentional**

An L&D professional at an
international credit company
explains that, for her company,
the three most important things
that the leaders can do to make
learning more intentional in
the organization is to 1) take
opportunities to share their
personal experiences and stories
with teams, 2) empower people to
learn from their mistakes, and 3)
make learning relevant by being
students themselves and putting
their own learning on display.

Actions like these shift mental
models about learning in the
organization and allow employees
to see the desired learning
behaviors demonstrated and
supported by leaders.

Culture Strongly Impacts Mental Models

Many of our interviewees talked about the increasingly global
nature of their work and its impact on their organizations and
workforce behaviors. Different geographies have different unique
norms and beliefs that strongly impact mental models about the
way work is done, how people interact, and how to best learn.
As companies become more global, extending products and
reaching for customers across geographical boundaries, people
must work across many cultures, an implicitly difficult task
the L&D team will likely have to manage. Although technology
solutions allow us to have direct and frequent contact with
others and learn collaboratively across the globe, they do
not solve all the inherent challenges. As such, it's critical to
identify, acknowledge, and accommodate those enduring, often
treasured, unique local cultural norms and shift beliefs toward a
more commonly shared global culture.

The Corporate Culture Influence

An organization's culture also has a strong impact on mental
models formed around expectations, values, and getting
work done. Effective workplace learning depends on a clear
understanding of the prevailing corporate culture. Is your
organization open to new ideas or slow to change? Is it casual
with regard to tradition or respectful of its history? What is your
organization's attitude about learning at work and with what
special language do you talk about it? Understanding and
incorporating these elements of corporate culture will increase
receptivity to learning.

STRATEGIES

Three strategies can help L&D professionals create learning
solutions that will impact learners' mental models. These will help
realize longer-term business goals:

- Intentionally use the action and reflection cycle to help
  people adapt their mental models

- Encourage storytelling to advance learning

- Foster a culture of learning across the organization

Intentionally Use the Action and Reflection Cycle to Help People Adapt Their Mental Models

As suggested in Principle 2, reflection is a critical element of
workplace learning. It is also key in helping to change mental
models. When reflection is incorporated into daily work routines,
people can gain insight into their mental models. Reflection ties
new experiences to existing frames of references (attitudes and

**Loyalty to the Team
More than the Organization**

A successful young marketing manager in a publishing company exhibits a behavior true to many millennials. Affiliated and loyal to those in his immediate marketing group, but distant and wary of the larger corporation, he consistently doubts the veracity of corporate policy announcements and changes. When "word" comes from headquarters, he expresses doubt to it being the "whole story" and he checks with trusted colleagues in Marketing to find out "what the rest of the story really is." While his distrust of the larger organization is evident, he regularly volunteers for extra work within the group, and takes visible pride in his and the marketing team's successes.

Management is challenged with how to reward the young manager's hard work and change his perception as to the larger corporation's motives and goals so both the employee and company can enthusiastically embrace his eventual transition to middle management. One strategy that is particularly effective in this situation is to "reward" the hard work by providing opportunities for the manager to work with other parts of the organization, in cross-functional learning programs or on projects that extend beyond his immediate group.

beliefs) while challenging attitudes and beliefs and preparing the individual for future experiences and related action steps. In this way, reflection becomes a support tool, allowing people to use their experiences as a springboard for learning and growth.

Encourage Storytelling to Advance Learning

Storytelling is an ancient art. A well-developed story can connect across age groups, convey communal attitudes and beliefs, and define corporate culture. Stories help learners identify with and adopt new ideas in a common, comfortable context. In turn, this can lead to behavior changes. In other words, stories are one of the fastest ways to influence people's point of view *and* their actions.

An effective story has a single theme, an organized plot, and raises questions that you, as the storyteller, will answer. Good storytellers pay careful attention to the intended audience (making the story line appropriate to the listeners), the style (using vivid word pictures, pleasing rhythms, and humor to convey the message), and the dramatic appeal (leaving an impression on the audience). How well someone tells the story will have a ripple effect on whether employees or learners embrace certain attitude or behavioral changes. Smart business leaders, such as Vittorio Colao, CEO of telecommunications giant Vodafone Group Plc., already understand this and put it practice on a regular basis. "I'm the storyteller of the company. There's nothing like telling anecdotes, indicating what you've seen, to create a desire to emulate and initiate contact," he told Forum during an interview.

Foster a Culture of Learning in the Organization

We talked earlier about the importance of fostering a culture of learning in the organization, but how do you do that? Certainly L&D encourages any and all learning opportunities. L&D can also make leaders, and the organization as a whole, more aware and sensitive to how people talk about learning at work. L&D professionals should also recognize that seemingly small things— like the way people refer to a learning opportunity or the social rewards they garner for sharing—contribute mightily to the culture of learning in the organization, and to the behaviors they exhibit.

Similarly, people's attitudes about their own learning impact their ability to acquire new knowledge. We've all heard people say they just cannot "do math," figure out spreadsheets, or that they are "hopeless" with computers. Learning requires a positive outlook. But learning also sometimes demands a deeper understanding of where these attitudes originate and of how strongly held beliefs shape workplace expectations.

Additionally, learning culture changes designed to shift attitudes, beliefs, and behaviors will have a powerful and sustained effect on the organization if its leadership puts these strategy suggestions into practice. If senior management not only encourages, but also participates in learning, the rest of the organization gets the message. It is important for leaders to make their own learning transparent. When leaders document and share their own instances of learning, even their failed experiments, they model the very behavior they hope to see in the workforce.

Leaders and L&D can, in these small and subtle ways, help generate the impetus for individuals and organizations to address learners' attitudes and beliefs.

Principle 4:

Provide Learners with a Balance of Challenge and Support

Principle 4: Provide Learners with a Balance of Challenge and Support

OVERVIEW

What was the biggest learning experience you had in your career? Chances are it was not the project that went perfectly, but rather the personally challenging situation you worked hard to overcome, or the timeline you struggled to meet. And, for the positive outcome, there was likely an individual who helped you get through the situation—a co-worker, a manager, or a friend who provided support and advice. When we stretch ourselves beyond what we think we can do, and get the just-in-time support we need, the learning experience is richer, more satisfying, and lasting.

"Challenge" is stretch learning: It's relevant to your job, but it's a reach for you. "Support," in a learning situation, does not mean sympathetic hand holding, but rather an environment where the learner can take risks and learn from failure. The best learning situations are those that provide a realistic level of challenge and enough support so that the learner feels comfortable asking for help when needed, understands that mistakes are an acceptable part of the learning curve, and is willing to keep pushing forward even when faced with uncertainty.

The dilemma inherent in this principle is: How can we create sufficient challenge, but still provide enough support?

RESEARCH FINDINGS

As already established, the reality of today's workplace is that learning, in most organizations, has moved closer to the work. For many, learning *is* the work. And, as work has become the place to learn, it becomes even more essential to construct work environments around the idea of maximized learning. A supportive and challenging work environment is the keystone to any successful learning implementation. The consensus from our interviews with experts is that learning is most effective when the learner is highly challenged. But they also caution that too much challenge is not a good thing. Stretch assignments are effective when they are doable, relevant, and the learner is supported. The trick to successful, enduring learning is to find the challenge/support sweet spot. Let's peel back the concept to see what this sweet spot looks like.

Let's say you're running to a meeting. In one scenario, imagine that you're heading to a "meet the client" meeting with a group of business leaders to discuss their business strategy and how you might help them achieve their objectives. Your colleague was originally scheduled to attend the meeting, but something more urgent came up and he asked if you take the lead since you had sat in on the kickoff call. He gave you his presentation files, and lent you his tie (it was casual Friday and you weren't expecting to have a meeting that day). You pull into the client's parking lot 5 minutes late because you forgot where to take a right turn. When you finally arrive

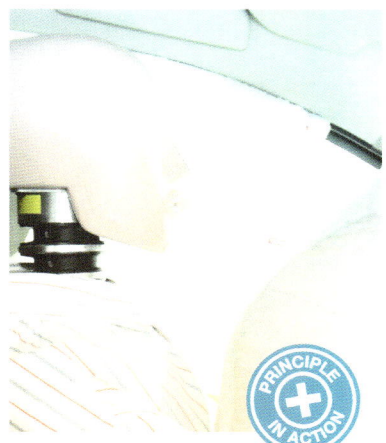

Practice with Safe Simulations

At a major energy company, the work is technical and high stakes. New employees ready to learn the critical competencies of more technically challenging, and potentially dangerous, energy generation must be supported as they learn. Understandably, these employees are nervous about the work ahead and realize these skills will be critical for their personal safety. To ease the employee's mastery of these new skills, leaders and L&D teamed together to devise highly realistic simulations. These 3D online simulated environments, rendered from detailed CAD drawings, allow technicians to acquire the skills they need in a safe and supportive learning environment.

at the meeting, you discover that, instead of the small group of five you were expecting, the large boardroom is set up for 30, and the group asks for your presentation so that they can display it at their quarterly department meeting. You can feel your adrenaline go up, right? It's a stressful situation, but one that is not conducive to learning about the needs of this group because the challenges lacked sufficient support.

Now imagine a different scenario. You are getting ready to meet with a key client in order to resolve one of their important business issues. This is your first face-to-face meeting, and you know that listening carefully, while providing value to the conversation, will be critical. You slept well the night before, your manager helped you prepare with a productive coaching session, there are a few reference items in your briefcase, and you are wearing your best suit. Your client greets you cheerfully and informs you that she's talked with the board of directors about your ideas. What's more, she has arranged for a member of the board to sit in on your meeting today since they think they'd like to move forward on your suggestions today. You take a deep breath and your brain kicks into high gear as you walk into the boardroom. This second scenario is the sweet spot to target in a learning situation. The employee was challenged enough to pay attention to new possibilities or sudden changes, but not overwhelmed by the task at hand. He benefited from the pre-design support structures and effectively responded to possible new challenges. As author David Rock puts it, learning organizations want to minimize the danger, but keep the challenge real.[8]

Additionally, a supportive environment includes an element of safety. In her article "The Competitive Imperative of Learning," Amy Edmondson, Novartis Professor of Leadership and Management at Harvard Business School, encourages organizations to create an environment of "psychological safety."[9] She describes this as a protected environment in which no one is penalized if they ask for help. This "safety net" is especially critical in businesses where knowledge changes constantly and workers often need to collaborate. She makes clear that creating a climate of psychological safety is independent of performance and accountability standards. In psychologically safe environments, workers fully understand their performance goals, are willing to offer up ideas, and ask questions. As Edmondson puts it, they are even willing to fail—and when they do, they learn.

Neuroscience shares further light on this principle. Challenging, but supported, situations create highly efficient learning patterns in the brain, while too much stress shuts it down (which ties to the discussion we raised in Principle 2). Challenge, which really translates to a little bit of manageable stress, is conducive for learning. That shot of adrenalin that comes from a deadline or a stretch goal can sharpen the senses and help with the learning

When It's Not Safe to Make Mistakes

An L&D professional at a major financial firm explained that getting the balance of challenge and support right is very difficult. "Some groups in our company have work that is so technical, and the importance of getting it right is critical. They just are not in an environment where it is ever safe to make mistakes. So we have to be very aware of that and understand the pressure that it creates." An effective way to support employees dealing with these daily pressures is to provide them with skills to manage their internal stress such as the reframing technique, which is a process for becoming aware of their negative thoughts so that they are able to change them.

process. However, too much stress has the opposite effect. We know that the brain region called the amygdala interrupts the functioning of the higher order regions of the brain (the frontal cortex) involved in learning and decision making. We also know that the amygdala is stimulated when we are under stress. So, it's an easy leap to say that our brains will function more optimally when we can limit stress. Of course, stress can't just be wiped away, but often we can reduce stress by reframing the issue or the situation. We reframe when we focus our attention on another element of the issue or decision.

STRATEGIES

This principle, perhaps more than any of the others, depends on leadership and first-line manager commitment to put it into practice. Managers are responsible for navigating the delicate balance between challenge and support, while providing their employees with the time, encouragement, and accountability for learning. What's more, the so-called sweet spot might be different for each employee, and effective managers will have to marshal various kinds of learning opportunities. The following strategies are positive models for leaders and managers. They are:

- Consider an apprenticeship model
- Integrate small experiments with feedback loops
- Embrace the fact that growth happens at "failure" points
- Combine elements of discovery learning

Consider an Apprenticeship Model

Benjamin Franklin began as a printer's apprentice to his elder brother. Henry Ford was a machinist apprentice before going on to launch Ford Motor Company. We're all familiar with the notion of a master and an apprentice, working together over time so that the apprentice can become a master in the given domain, thus training a new generation of workers on a particular skill.

But it's not just a good fit for printers and machinists of bygone years. This notion of apprenticeship plays equally well with knowledge workers in today's complex organizations. The time-tested model is very relevant and appealing in the new context of modern workplace learning. As the learning moves closer to the work and L&D expands existing challenge-support models, the idea of master working with apprentices is a good base to build off of, particularly when we consider that the master, or expert, does more than apply standard solutions to standard problems. They have internalized considerable knowledge and experience (see discussion of tacit knowledge in Principle 5) that they use to flexibly solve problems in real time, modeling much more than a

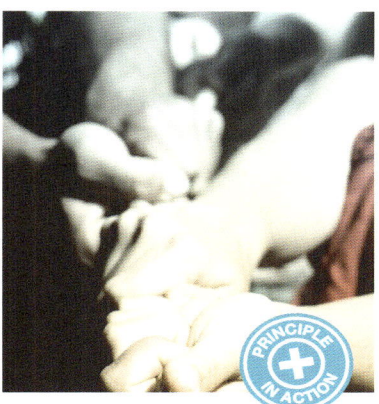

Working Together to Make It Work

One company, a limited liability corporation (LLC) owned by seven large, regional food service brokers, undertook the daunting task of working together to set industry standards and create common processes in order to meet their customers' needs.

As part of the consortium, member firms agreed to abide by majority vote, measure themselves in consistent ways, and use prescribed best practices to guide internal processes. Accomplishing these goals demanded major changes in behavior and skills upgrades so the seven presidents had to provide significant support to the meet the challenges they and their employees were expected to overcome.

For example, one challenge brought with it a substantial risk: The member firms agreed to be audited externally on specified progress metrics, and if a broker failed to meet the standards, it would be asked to leave the consortium. To support this challenge, the corporation invited key external consultant groups to help them create new practices and set up ongoing partnerships between the consultants and internal improvement teams. This fostered increased communication and credibility within the consortium and allowed for a better understanding of internal systems, company politics, and organizational culture.

specific skill in the process. A mentor's flexible problem-solving skills and his access to tacit knowledge provides a strong, safe, support net for learners grappling to work through the latest challenge before them.

An expert/apprentice relationship doesn't have to be a one-on-one commitment for months or years; it can be a project-specific arrangement for the short term, a single coaching session, or a job-rotation plan. And, a knowledge agent can mentor more than one apprentice at a time. Regardless of the arrangements, a properly functioning apprentice model creates and maintains the challenge and support sweet spot.

Integrate Small Experiments with Feedback Loops

One method managers can use to challenge their workforce and encourage growth is experimentation. The learning experts we interviewed advocate conducting many small business experiments in order to test new concepts, enter new markets, or try novel solutions. This method, like the rapid prototyping method we discussed in Principle 2, promotes an atmosphere of "safe" risk taking. Since many experiments are regularly being conducted, the risk with any one is minimized.

When conducting these experiments, it's important to build in a feedback loop—a clearly defined method for evaluating the experiment, determining what is and is not working, and how best to adjust it. Experimenting—or prototyping—rapidly in function areas where comments, constructive criticisms, and other relevant data can be gathered allows an organization to quickly size up a new opportunity and decide if it's worth pursuing.

As Christian Briggs, Instructor of New Media Theory at Indiana University School of Informatics, put it in our interview with him, "When an organization speeds up, it requires a greater degree of decentralization of decision making, a greater degree of experimentation, and shorter feedback loops in order to assess what is working and kill off what is not." In this way, new ideas are not halted or cancelled by the organization; they are selected, adjusted, (or killed) by the experiment.

Another intriguing way to think about conducting small experiments is to apply the approach to the idea of "hunches." Neuroscientists report that there is tremendous value in intuitive hunches or gut instincts. Literature on the subject refers to them as "pre-emptive knowledge" or "intuitive reckoning," which means that your brain might know something before you are conscious of it. Srini Pillay, a neuroscientist at McLean Hospital at Harvard University, strongly urges business leaders to listen to these hunches. "Business leaders can use their pre-emptive knowledge to influence and enhance their performance," Pillay told us during an interview. By reframing these instincts as a hypothesis, the hunch is put into the form of a question on which a small experiment can be run, and something everyone in the group can begin to test. It's a way for an organization to consider a new approach, without judgment, while giving everyone time to better understand it.

Whether rapid prototyping or turning hunches into experiments, these methods create safe, supportive environments in which to challenge employees.

Embrace the Fact That Growth Happens at "Failure" Points

Many of the business leaders and learning experts we spoke with agreed on one important observation—learning and growth happen at "failure" points. We put this word in quotations because, in this context, failures are not really failures. They are points where things did not work as expected and, therefore the place where the most learning can happen. Most often talked about in terms of sports analogies, we all know this strategy to be effective from our own experience. When we've been at the end of our rope, when we lost that big account, when we nearly failed— that's when we seem to learn the most. In reality, these "failure points" are "learning points."

Likewise, if learning is transparent throughout an organization, the failures, and what we learn from them, should also be transparent. In fact, that's where new social media tools can really assist organizations and anchor the learning support mechanism. By facilitating systematic, quick, and easy communications and constructive analyses of failures (through blogs, social networks, or other electronic communication methods), an organization can develop a regular rhythm of collecting and sharing insights and knowledge gleaned from these shortfalls.

Combine Elements of Discovery Learning

Discovery learning is a familiar educational philosophy rooted in the work of learning theorists Jean Piaget, Jerome Bruner, and Seymour Papert. It is an inquiry-based method where the learner draws on his or her own experience and prior knowledge to explore and manipulate new information, wrestle with questions, perform experiments, and construct new knowledge.

L&D professionals have embraced this method as learning shifts away from asking learners to sit passively in a classroom with an instructor pouring new information into their heads and moves toward an approach where the learner is in the driver's seat, figuring it out for him or herself. Of course, it's not as simple as just turning people loose with new information. In order to achieve the ideal challenge/support balance, the experience must be carefully planned and the right amount of scaffolding added as support; support can come from a facilitator of a learning experience, knowledgeable peers, an external coach, the employee's manager, or from the employee him or herself.

There are many advantages to this learning approach. When structured effectively, people feel more empowered by a discovery situation and are motivated to work harder. The most obvious advantage is that, with this method, the worker learns how to learn and can readily apply their skills to a new situation or problem.

Principle 5:

Create Opportunities for Participants to Teach as Well as Learn

Principle 5: Create Opportunities for Participants to Teach as Well as Learn

> "You have to get people to teach in order to learn. While you are transmitting, you are rethinking the information, reframing it for the audience and in doing so, you change the learning process."
>
> *Christian Briggs, Instructor in New Media Theory at Indiana University School of Informatics*

OVERVIEW

Learning consists of action (mental, physical, or both), and an opportunity to reflect on, or in, the action, a concept we introduced in Principle 2. People learn by doing, processing, and practicing what they have learned. Additionally, L&D professionals know that teaching is a particularly potent form of learning because it gives knowledge and learning more "stickiness," meaning that the more knowledge is shared with others, the more deeply reinforced it is into an individual's experience.

But it's not just the ongoing practice that makes teaching such an effective learning tool. In order to teach, learners must be intentional and articulate. They must dig deep and develop their own knowledge so that they can explain clearly and share it with someone else.

RESEARCH FINDINGS

The idea that we learn through teaching has been with us for a very long time. More than 2000 years ago, the Roman philosopher, Lucius Seneca coined the phrase, *docendo discimus*, translated as "we learn by teaching." More contemporary theories of learning tell us that one of the most powerful ways for K-12 students to learn is to teach. By teaching, students construct and deepen their own knowledge, become aware of gaps or missing information, and successfully shift the learned concept into their long-term memory.

The German language teacher and educational theorist, Jean Pol Martin, calls it "Lemen durch Lehren"—or learning by teaching. Martin writes compellingly about the way he turns his language classes over to students to do the teaching and his role shifts more toward midwife or facilitator. According to Martin, there is no better way for language students to recognize the holes in their own knowledge than to try to teach others.

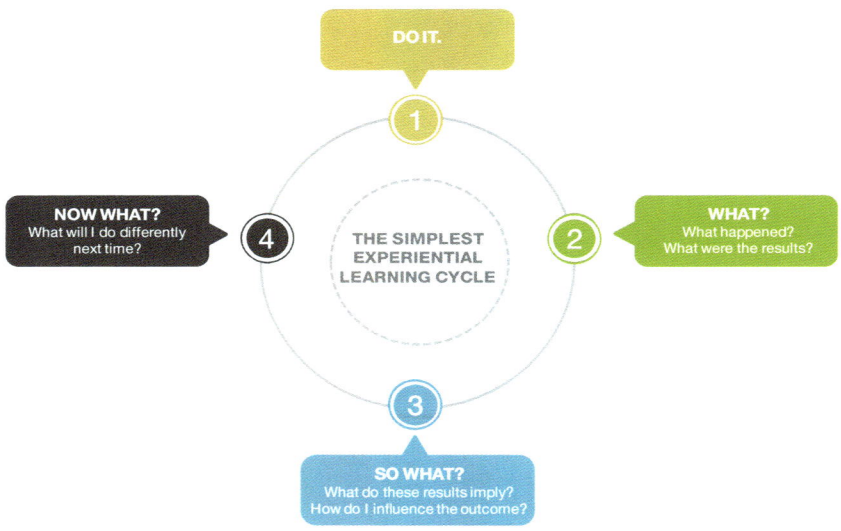

Knowledge Transfer Associates

To meet the demands of a 24-hour work schedule, a data management company created Knowledge Transfer Associates (KTA) to spread learning through the organization. KTAs are experts on a particular topic who are designated as the "go-to" person, the one to call on for help with that topic. They are embedded in the workforce, but they understand that part of their work hours are dedicated to teaching when called upon. To ensure that KTAs are successful, they are trained on how to be effective instructors and also receive coaching and support from their manager.

Support for the idea that teaching enhances learning can be found in the experiential learning model pioneered by educational theorist, David Kolb. Kolb's model consists of four elements: concrete experience (do it), observation and reflection (what?), the formulation of abstract concepts (so what?), and testing in new situations (now what?).

The last "now what?" step—testing knowledge in a new situation—is where the teaching comes in. When a learner becomes the teacher, he or she must recapture his own learning and evaluate it through the eyes of the person he will teach. Teachers have to determine whether his teaching strategy will be effective, what needs to be fine-tuned, and what learning elements are missing.

Dr. David Perkins, Senior Professor of Education at Harvard's Graduate School of Education, conducted research into what he terms "performances of understanding." Perkins and his colleagues carefully and systematically studied successful teachers and schools to identify what creates the awareness of the connection between individual pieces of information and allows knowledge to be put to use. Their findings center on what he calls a "performance perspective." Perkins explains that mastering a concept or a topic is measured by the degree to which a person can perform in a variety of thought-demanding ways, such as gathering evidence, finding examples, generalizing, demonstrating, or applying their understanding in a new way. What better way to "perform," or demonstrate one's understanding of a concept, than to teach it to someone else?

STRATEGIES

Teaching is a powerful learning tool, but not everyone in the organization is ready to just start teaching. You need to carefully select opportunities, prepare the "teachers," provide a scaffolding structure, and consider the context and people who will be "taught." The suggested strategies in this section, along with the tools listed in the Tool Kit, will help your organization increase the amount of effective teaching done by workers. They are:

- Include intentional teaching opportunities
- Use technology to enhance teaching
- Get used to blurred roles
- Increase the exchange of tacit knowledge

Include Intentional Teaching Opportunities

When L&D professionals design a learning program, they must incorporate strategic and intentional places for learner-as-teacher

Making Connections

Here at home, Forum began a new initiative to help connect learners to teachers. "The Connections Program" started with a questionnaire to be filled out by interested participants. On the questionnaire, people indicated what they were most interested in learning along with what knowledge they had to share. L&D program coordinators reviewed the completed questionnaires and made the matches. Learners were connected with teachers for an agreed upon period of time, meeting on a semi-regular basis, and supported with tools. Not only did the program connect learners with teachers but it also spawned a few communities of practice within the organization and nurtured new, unexpected relationships.

opportunities right into the learning deployment. This should be more than simply a "coaching check in" with a manager. L&D executives may want to ask people involved in a learning initiative to teach the material to their peers, to coach someone, or to capture their knowledge with the intent of sharing it. Intentionality is as important in teaching as it is with learning.

At the same time, it doesn't have to feel like an imposed requirement. It can be integrated as part of the daily workflow and experience. Charles Jennings, former CLO of Reuters and Thomson Reuters, has an interesting take on this concept. "We have to break the Plato mentality and return to Socrates. Socrates didn't see himself as a teacher. He had colleagues that he had conversation with," Jennings explained to us during an interview.

Use Technology to Enhance Teaching

You don't have to spend much time exploring the profusion of how-to videos on YouTube to draw conclusions about the way that technology facilitates a ready link between learners and their best teachers. The Web—through posted video, blogs, micro-blogs, wikis, and podcasts—makes it possible for anyone to do a little or a lot of skill-specific teaching. Consider incorporating the use of cheap, digital video cameras into the plan for your work and learning teams, document progress by maintaining a blog, and encourage communities of practice to use these tools for teaching others in their communities about their progress and results.

Get Used to Blurred Roles

A world where learners are teachers and teachers are learners can be disorienting. Most managers accept that part of their job is to teach, but how many of them fully understand their responsibility to learn? L&D can help organizations get comfortable with these ideas by working with leaders to model the desired practice, and encourage leaders to become leaders who both learn and make their learning visible to the organization.

Similarly, senior managers might need assistance getting used to the idea that leadership and "teachers" may come from unusual corners of the organization. Expertise in the workplace isn't really positional these days. Everyone is an expert on some topic, and it is up to the organization, its leaders, and L&D to identify where the necessary knowledge resides and to connect teachers to learners in a supportive way.

Increase the Exchange of Tacit Knowledge

There is an additional bonus to the strategic use of experienced, expert members or informed members of the organization to teach others—it helps capture, exchange, and spread tacit knowledge.

Tacit knowledge—or informal knowledge—is deeply embedded in an organization's operating practice and culture. It typically consists of habits, norms, values, relationships, intuition, and company history—all intangible and difficult to document. When people retire or leave an organization, tacit knowledge too often goes with them. Tacit knowledge, as opposed to explicit, or transactional, knowledge, is notoriously difficult to capture and transfer. One of the curiosities of tacit knowledge is that often, those who possess it do not realize it or do not appreciate how helpful it could be to others.

Managing tacit interactions requires different practices than traditional leadership or management. For this sort of knowledge exchange, an organization must think in terms of fostering connectivity, promoting networks, removing barriers, and facilitating learning rather than engineering connections or organizing events. In this way, an organization can increase the effectiveness and productivity of tacit interactions. When those with tacit knowledge are encouraged to teach, less experienced workers learn and the teacher reinforces his or her own learning—generating expanded capacity and skills for the organization as a whole.

Principle 6:
Design and Cultivate Learning Communities Along with Learning Media

Principle 6: Design and Cultivate Learning Communities Along with Learning Media

"As an organization, you need a structure that creates the broadest capacity for making connections."

George Siemens, Technology Enhanced Knowledge Research Institute (TEKRI), Athabasca University

What is a community? Dictionaries define it as a unified body of individuals with a common interest. In the workplace, a community can come in all shapes and sizes, and is often the basic functional unit of productivity performance in an organization. A community can be as small as a two-person project team or as large as a company; it can be simple or complex, with members meeting frequently or annually; it can bring people together online or face-to-face; and it can be short-term or designed around a mission that might last for years.

Throughout this document we use the term "community," but here we want to reinforce how it can go beyond a powerful concept and become a critical part of managing and integrating a multi-generational workforce. In a learning environment, communities, whether formally arranged or informally assembled, take collective responsibility for the learning of all members; they provide a structure where employees can assist one another as they master, or apprentice, a process, accomplish the work at hand, or reflect on successes or shortcomings. In other words, you can think of learning communities as a way to cultivate the experience that people have every day in the workplace.

RESEARCH FINDINGS

While communities are still evolving in the workplace setting, their impact is already being felt. Our research shows that community environments offer a particularly effective way to learn, and illustrate the concept "learning is the work." Based on our client experience, learning communities often become frameworks through which organizations can capture, cultivate, and build on the broader, collective experience. When people come together for a common purpose, they bring their experience and know-how with them; community structures provide the space where people can readily share their knowledge in a more immediate, interactive, and global way.

Compelling evidence for the importance of social interaction to learning comes from the landmark study of college and university students' experience by Richard J. Light, Walter H. Gale Professor of Education at the Harvard Graduate School of Education. Light discovered that one of the strongest determinants of students' success in higher education—more important than the details of their instructors' teaching styles—was their ability to form or participate in small study groups.[10] In the corporate world, learning communities serve as these small study groups, allowing members to share experience, information, and knowledge across geographic and organizational boundaries. These types of communities are increasingly being used to generate knowledge and strengthen employee skills.[11]

Form a Key Managers Group

In search of a way to groom future leaders at a major publishing company, senior management formed a community of middle managers to meet monthly with the president. Over time, the pro-forma meetings turned into working sessions where business problems could be debated, discussed, and vetted. After a year of regular meetings, the managers' group was charged with leading up a corporate organizational change effort. What started as a hood ornament group, turned into a mission-critical learning community for the company.

Participants in an effective learning community also tend to be committed to their group and that commitment drives their desire to work hard and help others, our findings indicate. A well-functioning learning community, for example, gives members an opportunity to achieve their personal learning goals while meeting the organization's requirements. In this way, communities could be a particularly good fit for millennials who thrive in smaller, local group settings but frequently resist larger corporate organizational constructs.

Likewise, cognitive anthropologists Etienne Wenger and Jean Lave propose that more effective learning takes place when learners are engaged in what they refer to as a "community of practice." Their definition of community of practice sounds very similar to the learning community that we just described: a group of collaborators, learning from each other and developing themselves personally in the process. As a community, they develop a shared repertoire of resources, experiences, stories, tools, and problem-solving techniques. With sustained interaction over time, they negotiate and institutionalize knowledge and meaning for their community—as well as the larger organization.

Our research and client interviews were clear: Communities are powerful knowledge networks. Whether you call them learning communities or communities of practice, forming them is a winning strategy to discover, aggregate, and share knowledge within your organization.

STRATEGIES

If learning communities are so powerful, why don't we form them all the time? In part, it is because it is not trivial to create a well-run and productive community. Challenges include: organizational barriers that prevent the appropriate community members from finding and connecting with each other; variable capacity among people for active membership in a regularly meeting community (or communities!); an ineffective mix of competencies among the membership, and a lack of organizational support. Here, we'll look at a few strategies to address these difficulties:

- Cultivate experience, cultivate communities

- Spark and support communities

- Recognize limitations

- Use media tools to support communities

Expertise in Unexpected Places

A customer service manager noticed that one of her representatives was a serious Twitter devotee, using it to keep in touch with family and friends. Looking for new ways to improve her company's customer service outreach, she suggested that he experiment with a Twitter ID for the company. Together, they formed a four-person community with two other interested reps. They set up a Twitter account and the Twitter devotee taught everyone how to use the tool. Within several months, the group gained a following as they groomed an active list of customers that they followed. Input gathered via the micro-blogging service was relayed to product development teams and used to shape new customer service policies in the department.

Cultivate Experience, Cultivate Communities

Learning and Development plays a crucial role in the formation, support, and stewardship of workplace learning communities. L&D provides the care and nurturing that moves a community from being a loose collection of people talking with each other to a well-oiled machine focused on performance improvements and stronger team relationships.

With the right support, L&D can transform a "work group" into a learning community with specific benefits to both the individual and the organization. For example, as the individual cultivates personal experience, expands his or her skills, and enjoys the team-centric connection, the organization benefits as the L&D group collects, archives, and shares learning results with the broader workplace. In effect, L&D sustains the community's process and performance data and brings it to the rest of the organization in an ongoing knowledge- and expertise-swapping environment.

Spark and Support Communities

Community and organizational leaders play a critical role in the success of a learning community, from the early forming stages right through to its conclusion. In the beginning stages, leaders will want to recruit and incentivize the community's membership, while establishing and communicating clear goals, expectations, and rewards. As the community gains traction, community leaders will be responsible for inspiring creativity, exploring new directions, holding the group accountable, and establishing milestones for evaluation and reflection. In the final phases of the community exchange, leaders will assist with an outcomes assessment, promote and share the community's work with others in the organization, and leverage the organizational culture change resulting from the effort.

As motivation, leaders often reward communities with the best performance. However, this practice can unfortunately backfire and encourage community members to hoard ideas and innovations rather than share them with a "competing" team. Leaders and L&D can best support their communities by offering incentives for absolute, as opposed to relative, performance, which helps ensure that the community's efforts are not in opposition to the overall organization's information-sharing goals. It is only when a community is a contributing part of the larger, overall effort that the individual *and* the organization benefit.

Smaller Hybrid Communities

One of the largest Internet portal providers promotes community-based action learning (learning-by-doing) by using a hybrid in-person/online model, offering two workshops, and creating two different-sized working groups.

The first workshop establishes the larger community's goals, conveys the principles of action learning, and sets up smaller peer-to-peer learning communities. These smaller communities, comprised of just two people, use the remainder of the first workshop to work together and think about partnering concepts and related advisory and reflection activities. Then, in-between workshops, the two-person communities practice self-directed action learning exercises individually and check-in with each other online for additional practice, feedback, and support with their community partner. The larger community conducts an online re-connect session midway before a second, final in-person workshop. At the second workshop, the action learning concepts are exhibited, discussed, and reinforced. The hybrid use of different learning and support practices makes the most of community initiatives at various levels.

Recognize Limitations

Leaders should recognize that workers may well be members of multiple communities, each with intense (and sometimes conflicting) demands. Community leaders should also note that not everyone has the same capacity or competency for this sort of group work and adjustments should be made accordingly.

If a community is formed by way of a formal learning event (a training program or a retreat), it is important to acknowledge the farther the community's work extends beyond the formal event, the harder it is to sustain. Steps must be taken to continue to motivate such a learning community while managing anticipated constraints.

Learning communities are not the solution for every workplace learning challenge, and some learning situations will need a different approach. For instance, sometimes didactic presentations are the best tool for the job, or, perhaps, a hybrid approach—where some of the learning is accomplished in classrooms, some in communities, some with web-delivered content, and some in isolation—will be effective. It is important to pick the right tool for the job and make a clear and explicit connection between the learning and the work.

Use Media Tools to Support Communities

A wide range of online tools can support community development and expansion. Social networking sites, blogs, wikis, communication mechanisms (that is, newsfeeds, alerts, forums, chat), and analytics can all facilitate the community's work and assist with data mining, aggregation, and archiving. But how do you decide which tools to use? Our experience shows that it's less about the tool than what the tool can do for you. The first step is to identify what you want individuals and the organization to gain from your learning communities. Then look at your current tools and identify gaps—what they cannot currently do for you that you need done. From there, focus on filling the requirement gaps. When suggesting options, emphasis should be placed on the *affordances* of the tools (what they can do better than some other tool) rather than the specific tool itself.

Conclusion

"Content can be googled, but context is king. It is amidst the fast-paced demands of the workplace that performance improvement is required in pursuit of business goals. This is where individuals and teams interact and work—this is the future of workplace learning and the future home of L&D."

Elizabeth Griep, VP, Advanced Workplace Learning, The Forum Corporation

Despite our best guesses, we're still living in an uncertain business world. No one really knows how deeply the millennials will change a company's learning footprint or what new technologies will be available. Geographically, different regions will also likely see cross-generational trends crop up at different times, and maybe even in completely different ways. Culturally, too, organizations will have to match learning strategies against what best fits their business models and organizational climate. And, of course, it will take time—and future hindsight—to really see how these shifts fully played out and what the outcomes were.

Even so, we can be sure that a company's focus on learning and its capacity to flexibly adjust learning tools and techniques to meet the changing demands of its workforce will affect business performance, speed, and competitiveness. In what's becoming a general truism, continuous learning creates sustainable business advantages, and successful companies constantly seek out innovative ways to cultivate learning.

Advancing
Performance Tool Kit

Tools for L&D Professionals

Tools for L&D Professionals

In the book Strategic Speed: Mobilizing People, Accelerating Execution the authors identified that companies with leaders who "cultivate experience" outperform companies that don't, even through a recession. No surprise here—as L&D professionals, this is a principle that we have been screaming from the mountain top for our entire careers. In the research we conducted for this report, we talked with experts and with practitioners about what cultivating experience looks like from an organizational perspective and, combined with Forum's 35+ years of experience, we put forward this definition: Cultivating organizational experience is the discipline of creating the systems that generate significant and shared learning about an organizational issue or skill that can be harnessed to achieve business results.

The six principles of workplace learning outlined in the research report section can be applied not only to learning program design but to the design of learning architectures. Calling on our 35+ years of experience delivering business results through learning for clients, we created this tool kit to provide you with the tools and processes for developing organizational learning systems that cultivate experience. While these tools and processes can be expanded, we recommend that you consider what is provided here as the minimum, as the magic lies in the entire system and how it works together. It is often tempting to skip a step or take a short cut in the interest of saving time, effort, or money. Our advice to you is—don't!

The process begins once a business opportunity or challenge is presented and, in order to achieve success, some degree of behavior change must take place.

Why?

Articulating the business opportunity or challenge in terms of impact on the organization will both inform your approach and establish the business metrics that your solution needs to deliver. Without specifying the results that need to change, the whole effort can take a completely different (and erroneous) trajectory.

How?

Two macro steps clarify the purpose of the solution:

Step 1: Identify stakeholders
Step 2: Clarify stakeholder expectations

Stakeholder Map

A stakeholder is any individual or group you will need to collaborate with to achieve the learning priority. This begins with the person (or persons) who have initiated the need, such as a senior executive or the head of a functional group like Sales. In addition to the sponsor, however, stakeholders also include the people who will provide you with the resources, information, and expertise you need to develop and implement a successful learning initiative. Completing a Stakeholder Map can help you identify the people you need to involve to varying degrees and in varying capacities while creating your approach.

Stakeholder Map

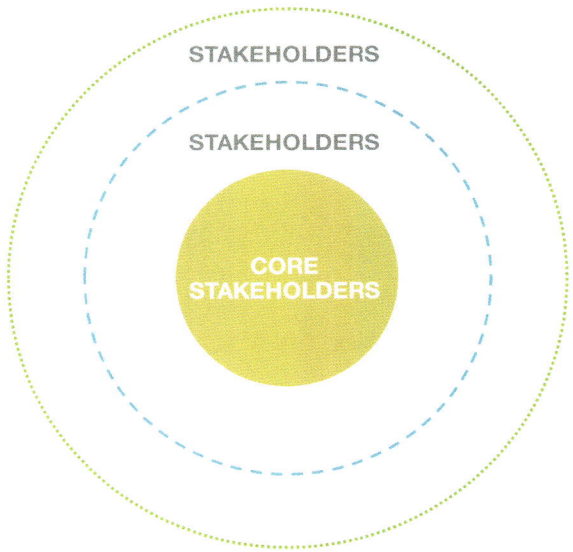

1. In the center circle of the diagram, write the names of those who have a direct interest in the business issue and the potential solution—this could include a sponsor, a business leader, and/or a part of the target audience. The stakeholders identified here are those for whom the solution is highly work-relevant and/or for whom the success of the solution is *essential*.

2. In the middle circle, write the names of stakeholders who are indirectly impacted by the business issue and the potential solution. Examples of people who may be represented here are other L&D professionals as well as managers or direct reports of those targeted for the learning.

3. In the outer circle, write the names of stakeholders who are peripheral to the business issue and potential solution. This would include, for example, leaders of other business units, support personnel, faculty, systems managers.

Stakeholder Expectations Protocol

Referring to the Stakeholder Map, use the protocol below to guide conversations with stakeholders from the various levels to gain further clarity on the business issue, potential solution requirements, and the scope of the solution.

- What is the business issue to be addressed?

- What is the objective of the learning solution?

- What does success look like from a business perspective? (increased revenue, reduced time-to-market, increased customer satisfaction?)

- What is the current state?

- How are you currently addressing this issue?

    — What has worked?

    — What has not worked? Why?

- What do people need to do differently to meet the objective(s)?

- What actions need to be taken to reach the objective?

    — From an organizational perspective? (for example, do organizational structures need to change?)

    — From a process perspective? (for example, will this require process re-engineering?)

    — From a leadership perspective? (for example, what do leaders and managers need to do?)

    — From an individual perspective? (for example, what are the new skills and behaviors needed?)

- What are the results expected to be seen?

- What are your measures?

- Who will observe and confirm the desired changes? When? How often?

DEFINE THE AUDIENCE

Why?

The background of your target audience and the environment they live and work in impacts the effectiveness of various learning methods. Take time to identify the characteristics of your audience to ensure the methodologies employed will facilitate the learning rather than impede it. Four things to consider regarding your audience are:

- Generational influences

- National culture

- Organizational culture

- Organizational role/level

How?

Use the areas below to help you explore the various aspects of your audience and develop a solution that meets the needs of your audience.

Generational Influences

Consider the target audience and determine where future participants fall in the generational profiles below. Multi-generational audiences require a more robust combination of learning methodologies, so it is critical to determine the generational mix up front and identify which approaches you should incorporate to meet all learners' needs.

Give Me What I Need

	VETERAN (born before 1946)	BOOMER (1946-1964)	X'ER (1965-1981)	MILLENNIAL (1982-2000)
STYLE	Formal	Semiformal	Not so serious; irreverent	Eye-catching; fun
CONTENT	Detail; prose-style writing	Chunk it down but give me everything	Get to the point — what do I need to know?	If and when I need it, I'll find it online
CONTEXT	Relevance to my security; historical perspective	Relevance to the bottom line and my rewards	Relevance to what matters to me	Relevance to now, today, and my role
ATTITUDE	Accepting and trusting of authority and hierarchy	Accept the "rules" as created by the Veterans	Openly question authority; often branded as cynics and skeptics	Okay with authority that earns their respect
DESIRED LEARNING APPROACH	Traditional, instructor-led, reading, homework, "teach me"	Traditional, group effort, expert driven, self-driven "lead me to information"	Teamdriven, collaborative, "wisdom of crowds," peer-to-peer, "connect me to people"	Give context and meaning, make it fun, search and explore, entertain me, "connect me to everything"
SPEED	Attainable within reasonable time frame	Available; handy	Immediate; when I need it	Five minutes ago
FREQUENCY	In digestible amounts	As needed	Whenever	Constant

National Culture

While national cultures seem to blur in global organizations (sometimes to the point where organizational culture appears to replace national culture) it is important to give thought to the various national cultures that may exist within your target audience. For example, "Europe" is not one culture but rather a continent comprised of many nations and therefore many national cultures. Therefore, learning design and methodologies that work in France will not always work in Germany. For example, *in general,* the French love conversation and debate, often talking over one another, so group discussions are a great learning approach. Germans, on the other hand, *in general,* are more formal and value facts and details, which means they prefer lectures. These differences influence preferred learning design and methods.

Forum has extensive global experience and, as a result, has identified best practices for developing solutions that will extend across national and/or cultural groups. At the core of these best practices are the creation of a global design and implementation team who will:

- Develop a thorough understanding of key stakeholders and participants and their unique global context

- Identify areas for strategic consistency and opportunities for adaptation at the local level

- Develop a clear plan for how to involve senior management in shaping, reinforcing, and removing barriers

- Gain agreement on the global implementation plan

Numerous tools and web sites are available that provide information about cultural dimensions. One such approach is the framework created by Geert Hofstede™ which can be found on the web at *http://www.cyborlink.com/besite/hofstede.htm*. Research your audience's national culture, avoid assumptions, and then keep these cultural differences in mind as you build your solution.

Organizational Culture

Organizational culture is defined by some as the observed customs, rites, ceremonies, stories, and beliefs within an organization or part of an organization. Others define it as the conscious beliefs that influence employees' attitudes and behaviors. Regardless of how you define it, the organizational culture of your audience plays a significant role in determining what will be most effective in achieving lasting behavior change.

A number of tools and formal assessments can be used to gain a complete understanding of your organization's culture. One tool, the Dennison Culture Survey,[12] provides a link between organizational culture and many of the bottom-line performance measures that learning solutions seek to impact (such as profitability, quality, innovation, market share, sales growth, and employee satisfaction).

Organizational Role/Level

In addition to your audience's generational influences, and national and organizational culture, each participant group's role and level in the organization will impact how they learn. Use the table below to identify the typical needs and concerns of your audience by role/level. Consider how the needs and concerns outlined might need to influence learning methods used (also remember to refer to this information during design). Then, combine what you know about role/level with what you have identified in the other areas of generational influences, national culture, and organizational culture.

Role/Level	Needs & Concerns
Individual Contributors	Emphasis on self-management
	Development of technical proficiency
First-Level Managers	Focus most of their time on tactical, management activities
	Focal topics are operational, including delegating, budgeting, and staffing
Mid-Level Managers	Focus equally on all three categories: management, leadership, business strategy
	Focal topics include communications, team building, coaching, and motivating
Senior-Level Managers	Focus has an increased emphasis on leadership and business strategy
	Decreased emphasis on operational skills
Executives	Primary focus on running the business
	Focal topics include strategic planning, business acumen, value creation

DEFINE THE LEARNING ARCHITECTURE

Why?

A clearly defined overarching approach enables you to identify and build the various individual solutions and surrounding structures required to ensure that the learning leads to results.

How?

Using your clarified business opportunity or challenge, and your defined audience, work with appropriate stakeholders to:

- Review current developmental activities/interventions that support resolution of the business opportunity or challenge (if any).

- Of those, determine which are effective and which are not. Note cases where content applies, but learning methodology needs to change.

    - *See Current Offering Assessment below*

- Identify offering gaps, then prioritize both existing and future gaps by audience level

- Determine appropriate learning architecture

    - *See Learning Architectures Tool below*

- Apply appropriate mix of learning methodologies within the architecture, given audience

    - Be sure to include sustainment activities in all curriculum offerings (*see section on "Develop an Execution Strategy"*)

    - Use a mix of event-based learning, sustained learning, and integrated learning (*see section on "Build the Blended Curriculum and Solutions"*)

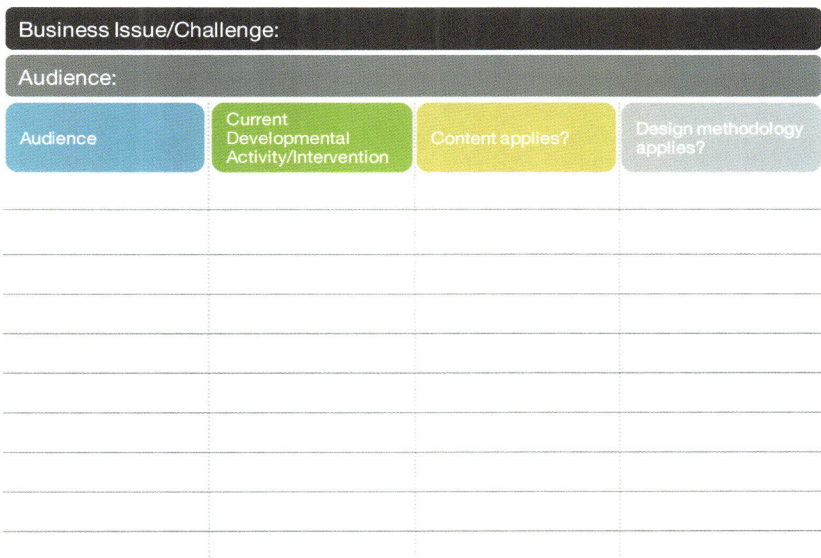

Business Issue/Challenge:			
Audience:			
Audience	Current Developmental Activity/Intervention	Content applies?	Design methodology applies?

Learning Architectures

Use the matrix below to determine which learning architecture best suits the need of your curriculum. Note, depending on the business issue or challenge and the audience levels involved, the most effective architecture for your curriculum might include a combination of these.

Learning Architectures Tool

Learning Strategy	Purpose
Personal Development	Provide individuals with easy, flexible, inexpensive access to self-paced learning
Corporate Initiative	Provide a baseline of understanding and skill required to support the strategy
Functional Academy	Provide an intensive experience where participants learn functional skills and are socialized into a role (such as Sales and IT)
Executive Development Program	Provide a process for grooming future leaders and communicate a management philosophy
Learning Intervention	Solve a business problem by providing learning opportunities tied to a specific situation and need

Why?

For two of the four trends identified by the research as impacting learning in today's workplace—bringing learning closer to the work; and making sense of the growing number of available learning tools—blended learning is an obvious solution. Also, by applying a blended approach to learning design, you will be able to more effectively incorporate the principles of workplace learning.

How?

Intentionally blend your learning on multiple levels: across the contexts, using multiple interaction and delivery methods, and over time.

Learning Fan

Forum's learning fan reflects the contexts, multiple methods available, and the importance of learning over time. This tool provides a holistic way to explore the various elements of a blended learning solution.

Forum's Learning Fan

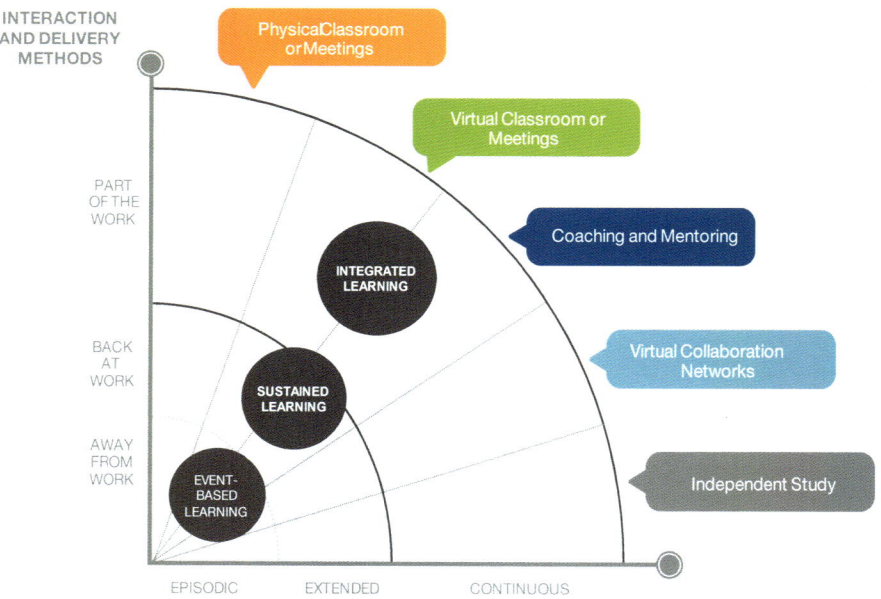

Three Learning Contexts

- *Event-based learning*: formal, expert, research-based courses, workshops, curricula, executive sessions, or large-group events to convey knowledge and develop capabilities.

- *Sustained learning*: formal and informal processes where the concepts/skills learned in a formal setting are reinforced and applied on the job.

- *Integrated learning*: real-time work experiences leveraging the knowledge and experiences of others or exploring new ways to improve performance. These experiences, while often perceived as being informal, can be formalized through the use of social media tools, performance support, and communities of practice.

Five Learning Methods

- *Physical classroom or meetings*: Synchronous sessions where learners come together in the same physical location.

- *Virtual classroom or meetings*: Using web conferencing, small groups participate in a series of synchronous interactive sessions led by a facilitator.

- *Coaching and mentoring*: Formal and informal coaching processes where expert coaches assess, challenge, and support learners to develop targeted capabilities. Coaching and mentoring can occur one on one or one on group, virtually or face to face, synchronously or asynchronously.

- *Virtual collaboration networks*: A primarily asynchronous approach to learning, this method employs a variety of technologies to deliver learning to a distributed audience. This method can incorporate all of the other learning methods to yield a highly blended solution. Facilitators drive the learning using virtual classrooms, social networking tools, and rich media presentations over a period of time. In some cases, e-learning tutorials may be incorporated.

- *Independent study*: as the title implies, this asynchronous method involves individual learning items such as tutorials, reading assignments, and podcasts to provide information to learners.

Over Time

In order to achieve lasting impact, it is necessary to plan how the learning system will extend and evolve over time. That is, what are the elements that need to be imbedded into the system to ensure that learning acquired in a formal setting is applied back on the job and then improved upon or enhanced through continued learning as part of the work? Without this "over time" element, learners are significantly less likely to retain or apply what they've learned regardless of how engaging the developmental activity or intervention might have been.

Three different examples of blended approaches are depicted in the following graphics. Each example illustrates a possible solution-level response (not curriculum) to the same issue—developing a leadership pipeline—but the difference among them is in their learning context (event-based, sustained, integrated). The organization would need to choose the blended approach to this particular solution based on the definition of their business opportunity/challenge, their definition of their audience, and their overall learning architecture.

OPTION 1
Emphasizes Event-Based Learning

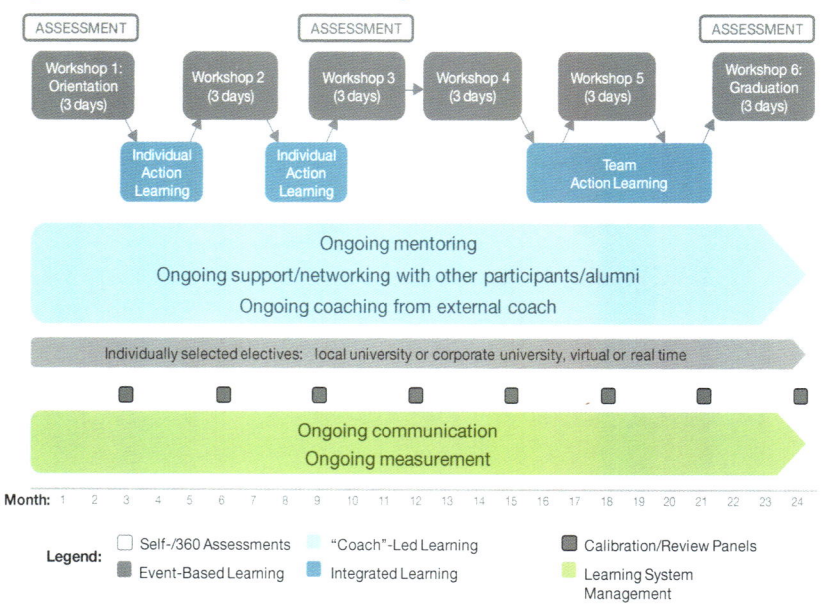

OPTION 2
Emphasizes Sustained Learning

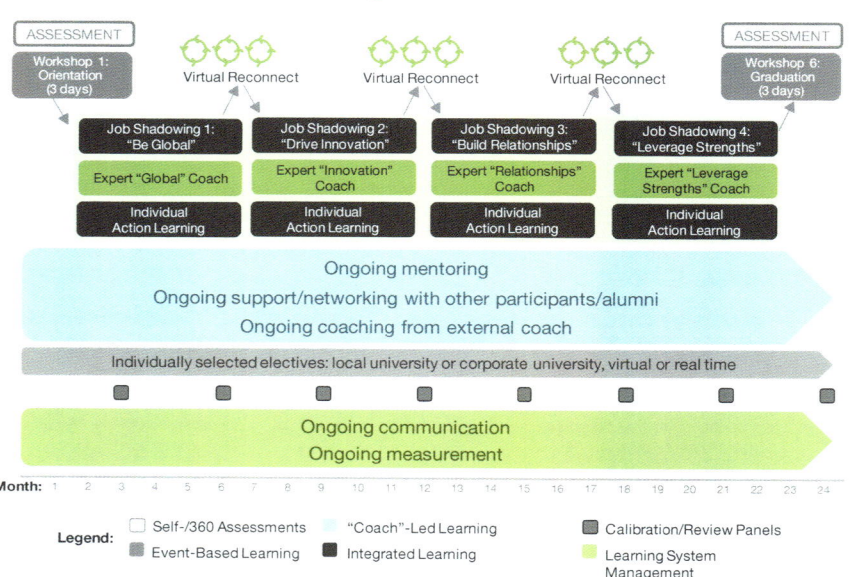

OPTION 3
Emphasizes Integrated Learning

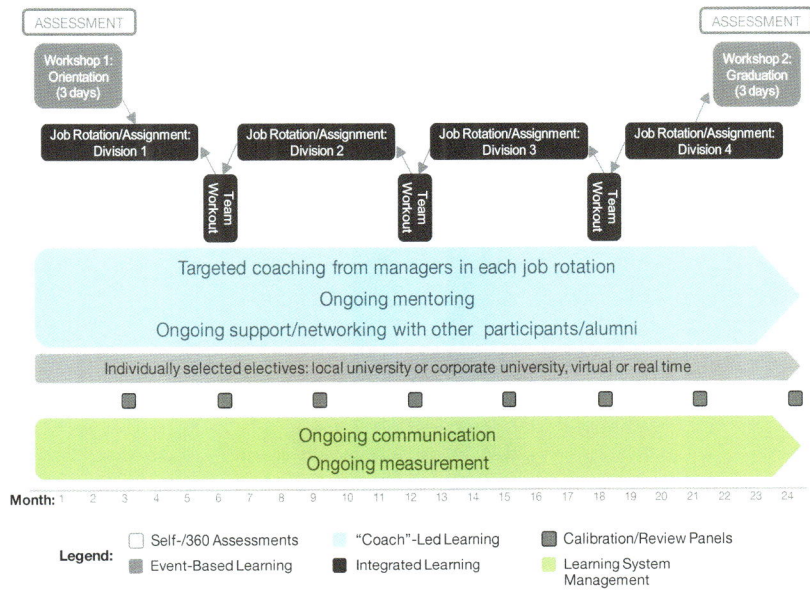

We have all heard the phrase "build it and they will come" and up to this point we have been focused on building the learning architecture. This is only one - third of the task. Equally important are designing the learning experience and developing a strategy for execution. Techniques for designing the individual learning experiences within a curriculum can be found in the next section, Tools for Designers.

DEVELOP AN EXECUTION STRATEGY

Why?

The execution strategy is a key secret to ensuring that learning—whether it is knowledge, skills, attitudes, or behavior—is fully integrated into work.

How?

Forum's research shows that successfully executed learning initiatives consistently include:

- A comprehensive communications strategy

- A sustainment strategy

- An impact measurement strategy

Communications Strategy

This Communications Process Tool will help you plan for superior communications that support your learning initiatives. The process can be customized to best fit the content and scale of your project—from individual learning activities or interventions to a full curriculum.

This tool gives you an overview of:

- Stakeholders, or those most often involved in some part of communications planning, along with their responsibilities.

- Steps to take to drive the learning initiative through its life cycle:

    - The *Align* phase, planning the activities that lead up to the learning initiative

    - The *Equip* phase, organizing the communications activities that take place during the learning events

    - The *Sustain* phase, maintaining the momentum you built by achieving your organization's goals through learning

Communications Process Tool

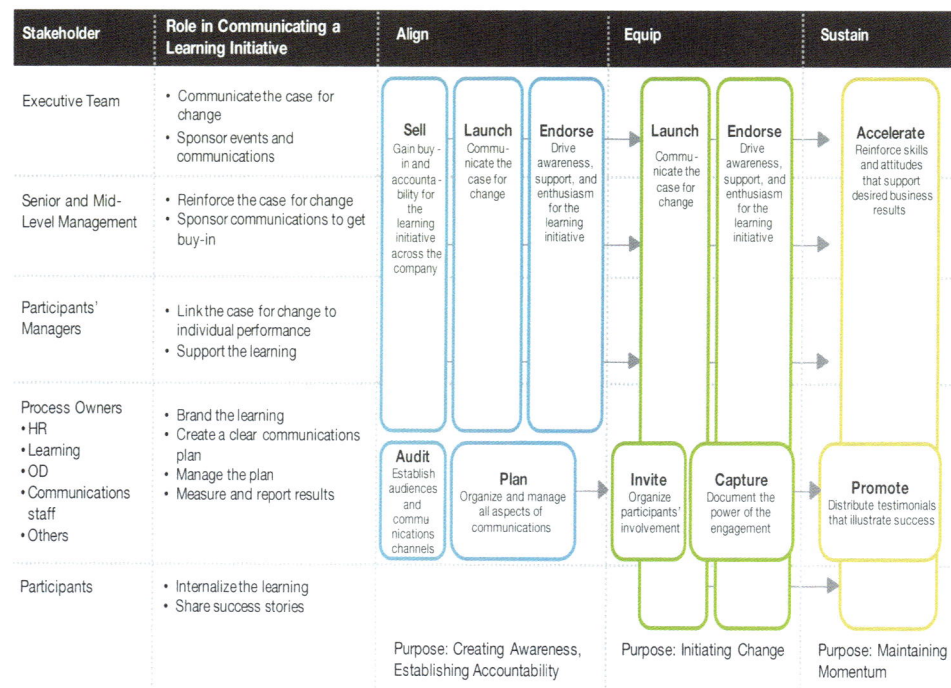

This Communications Process Tool works hand-in-hand with Forum's Communications Tool Kit, which provides practices and tools to support your communications strategy.

Sustainment Strategy

Equally important to building the solution is planning for sustainment. As L&D professionals, we know all too well that learning and development interventions often focus solely on the primary learning experience, or the main event. Ongoing reinforcement of the new knowledge and behavior is often neglected, to the detriment of real and lasting impact.

Our experience shows that for these plans to be successful, they need to fit with the learning environment, with the nature of the work, and with the work styles and capabilities of the target audience. Steps for defining an effective sustainment strategy include:[13]

- Assess the learning environment. Consider:
  - What learning practices, processes, and tools are currently used to reinforce learning? Be sure to look at what happens both formally and informally at the organizational, work group, and individual level.

- Identify the right owners. Consider:
  - Who officially or unofficially drives the learning in your organization and for the audience in question? (See *Three Ownership Levels Tool*, below.)

- Choose sustainment activities to fit the learning environment and the ownership level. Taking ownership level into consideration, review the categories of possible sustainment activities and determine which would be most effective to incorporate to ensure long-term integration of knowledge and behaviors. (See the Sustainment Activities Tool, below.)

Three Ownership Levels Tool

Determine which of the following three situations most accurately describes the current learning (both formal and informal) for your audience:

The learning for this organization/audience is:	Owner/ driver:
Centralized within a function (such as L&D, or Sales), creating a push out to the organization or target audience	Organization-driven
Led by leaders/managers of the target audience through modeling, coaching, and requiring the learning of their employees	Leader-driven
Initiated by individuals who find opportunities and support for their own learning and network	Learner-driven

Sustainment Activities Tool

In our experience and work with clients who take the "sustain to attain" (versus the "spray and pray") approach to performance improvement, there are four categories for sustainment activities. The map below illustrates the types of sustainment activities available in each category (defined below) across the three levels of ownership.

Refer to your learning environment assessment results, and given your determination of primary ownership, select a combination of applicable activities.

Specific Sustainment Activities by Ownership Level

	ORGANIZATION DRIVES	LEADERS LEAD	LEARNERS SEEK
EXAMPLES: "Show It"	Refreshers / Reconnects/Result Stories / Expert Demonstrations	Leader-Led Skills Clinics / Results Stories / OTJ Demonstrations	Job Aids/Tool Kits / Reference Materials / Role Models
ASSESSMENTS: "Need It"	360 Behavior Surveys / Impact/Application Survey / Business Case	180 Behavior Surveys / Manager Observations / Coaching Conversations	Self-Assessments / Active Reflection / Requests for Feedback
OPPORTUNITIES: "Do It"	Action Learning / Temporary Assignments / Leading Learning Assigmnts.	Delegation / Stretch Assignments / Team Projects	Goals/Action Plans / Deliberate Practice / Requests for Assigmnts.
SUPPORTS: "Grow It"	"Coach on Demand" / Communities of Practice / Recognition Awards	OTJ Coaching / After-Action Reviews / Recognition	Self-Coaching / Peer Support / Informal Mentors

Examples ("I See It"): Activities in this group help learners see and know what they should be applying back on the job. These activities demonstrate and show people what successful application of the behaviors looks like. They provide relevant and regular examples, in a structured way, over time, to help learners see clearly what it looks and feels like to successfully master the new behaviors and tools.

Assessments ("I Need It"): Assessment activities uncover gaps in performance and opportunities for improvement. These activities allow the learner, line manager, coach, and organization to rate current performance and then use the feedback to establish and/or update improvement goals.

Opportunities ("I Do It"): Deliberate practice is at the heart of behavior change. Opportunities for application of new skills and tools don't have to amount to "10,000 hours" but they do need to be more significant than a couple of notes in an action plan at the end of a formal workshop or e-learning event. The nature of the work determines to what extent deliberate practice needs to be in a safe or simulated environment or whether practice drills can be done on the job.

Supports ("I Live It"): Activities in this group include significant catalysts for change. Affirmation and encouragement are often underrated but have been shown to be highly significant in helping people to make a change in behavior and move through any short-term performance dip on the way to lasting performance improvement.

For more information on sustainment see Forum's point of view paper, Behaviors Changes That Stick.

Impact Measurement Strategy

Enhancing business impact requires thinking about measuring as more than just collecting data; it's equally important to think of it as a process of communicating findings to others in a way that demonstrates success and identifying ways to increase impact. Measuring needs to be grounded by a solid plan that addresses four elements:

Focusing: The purpose of the focusing phase is to align measurement activities to address the needs/expectations of multiple stakeholder groups identified in Clarify the Business Opportunity or Challenge step. The focusing phase grounds measurement activities in a thorough understanding of three things:

- Purpose: Why was the initiative undertaken? What problem is it trying to solve?

- Stakeholders: Who cares about the results of the initiative? What do they care about?

- Impact model: How is the learning component of the initiative expected to influence business results?

Discovering: The discovering phase is a reality test. Its purpose is to collect the best available evidence in order to judge whether the learning initiative yielded the desired results. Typically, the discovering phase focuses on three areas:

- The learning experience (such as a workshop)

- On-the-job application (such as leading more effective meetings and conducting more effective sales calls)

- Business results (such as increased revenue, improved project results, and increased customer loyalty)

Discovering also aids in understanding what actually happened and determining what actions to continue taking and what actions to stop taking, in order to increase impact. The discovering process considers:

- Metrics: For each type of impact, ask, "What do we need to measure to determine whether this happened?"

- Methods: "What is (are) the most credible and efficient research method(s) to use?"

- Data collection plan: "Who is responsible? What's the timing? What output is expected?"

Proving: The next two phases, proving and improving, are critical—but often neglected. They involve reporting to stakeholders about changes that have been made (proving impact) and ways to increase the impact of the initiative based on what has been learned (improving impact). Since they both address related questions, the two phases are often undertaken at the same time and place, for example, in a debrief meeting that follows a pilot program.

The process of proving includes, but is not limited to, formal presentations, working sessions, and one-on-one dialogues or small-group meetings that consider the effects of the initiative and ways to enhance the positive effects. Key considerations in the proving phase are:

- Audience: Which stakeholder group is involved? What are its expectations, and what data is available to address them?

- Method: Is it a formal presentation? An opportunity for dialogue and brainstorming?

- Framework: In what form should the findings be presented? What story do the findings tell?

Improving: Any large-scale initiative, no matter how well-conceived and implemented, can be improved. Likewise, no initiative misses the mark so disastrously that it yields no positive effects at all. Too often, however, participants fail to learn and apply the initiative's lessons. Every initiative is, by nature, an experiment. The improving phase aims to derive maximum value from the experiment: to build on what works and eliminate what doesn't. Factors to consider in improving impact are:

- Leadership: What can leaders do to reinforce and extend the value of the initiative (provide coaching and tools, or recognize and reward success, for example)?

- Human Resources support: How can HR systems, such as performance management, better support the initiative?

- Learning team: How can the learning experience be enhanced? What additional learning or support is needed?

CONCLUSION

This tool kit was created with the goal of assisting L&D professionals with some useful baseline processes and tools to get started in articulating a learning system that addresses business challenges and brings lasting results to the organization. Forum's 35+ years of experience in delivering business results through learning for our clients has led to a wealth of additional breadth and depth in developing organizational learning systems that cultivate experience.

Tools for Designers

The Learning Approaches Model

- To expand designers' thinking about various learning goals and learning approaches

- To help designers match learning goals to the best learning approaches

The Learning Approaches Model

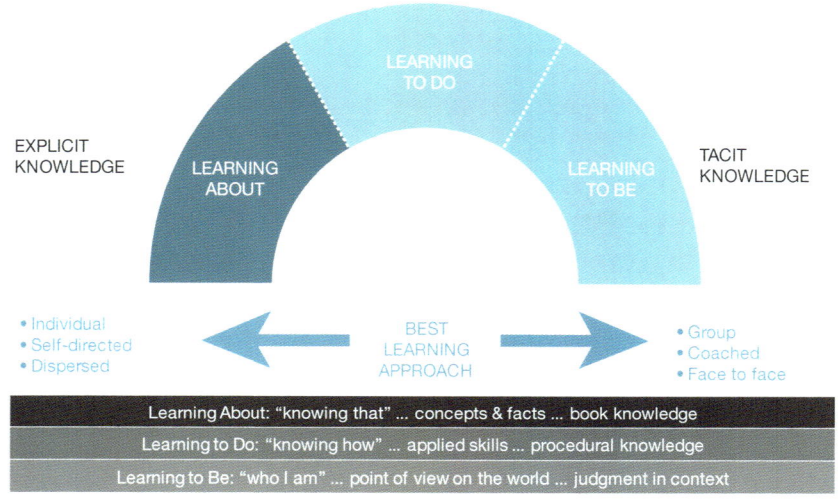

THE MODEL

Types of Learning Goals

Psychologists and learning theorists have said that knowledge can be categorized into two types: explicit and tacit. Explicit knowledge is articulated or spelled out, like the knowledge written down in a strategy book or how-to manual. Tacit knowledge, on the other hand, has an implicit, unarticulated quality. Tacit knowledge is associated with practical (as opposed to academic) intelligence. Someone with tacit knowledge can apply good judgment in complex conditions, perhaps without being able to say exactly which rules he or she is following.

Today's workplace requires the exercise of both explicit and tacit knowledge. Reading a book on negotiation strategy and being able to pass a test on the knowledge captured therein are not enough to make you a master negotiator.

Forum's Learning Approaches Model divides the continuum from explicit to tacit knowledge into three broad learning goals: learning about, learning to do, and learning to be.

Learning about is what you do when you read books, look at examples, and listen to lectures. It means absorbing explicit knowledge. An example would be a music lover who reads books and music reviews, goes to concerts, takes classes in music appreciation, listens to CDs, and can talk intelligently *about* music styles, instruments, and history.

Learning to do is in the middle of the explicit-tacit continuum. It is procedural knowledge: being able to describe and demonstrate certain procedures, processes, or skills and to produce certain deliverables. In the music example, someone who has "learned to do" would be taking lessons in an instrument and be able to *play* music— for example, in recitals or for his or her own entertainment.

Learning to be is far over on the tacit side of the continuum. Learning to *be* a musician requires the kind of dedication, experience, and development of judgment that is sometimes called professionalism. It also requires the development of a particular point of view, a way of relating to the world. One would expect someone who has learned "to be" to be able to exercise a complex, intertwined set of knowledge, skills, and attitudes at any given moment—and to do it in a highly individual manner. As Davenport and Prusack say, "The distinctive style of a master musician can barely be described in words, much less externalized in a way that would allow someone else to play in an identical way."[14]

There is a characteristic question for evaluating each learning goal:

- Learning about: Do they *know more?*

- Learning to do: Do they *perform better?*

- Learning to be: Do they *see things differently?*

We envision these three learning goals as forming an arch. The middle of the arch (learning to do) is the goal people usually focus on when it comes to teaching (especially given the workplace emphasis on performance and behavior change). It is important, however, to think about all that needs to be learned and to tease out both the more explicit (learning about) and the more tacit (learning to be) aspects of the desired learning.[15]

Appropriate Learning Approaches

Different learning goals demand different learning approaches. Depending on whether the learning goal leans toward tacit or explicit knowledge, the best learning approach will be either group-based, coached, and face to face; or individual, self-directed, and dispersed.

Why is bringing people together so important to the transmission of tacit knowledge? Davenport and Prusack point to two reasons. One is that tacit knowledge is too subtle and complex to transmit fully in words; one needs to "see how it's done." The other reason, at least as important, is that *trust* is essential to persuading people to change their behavior. Why would some words on a computer screen convince you that there is a better way to do something you have been doing for years? You need a chance to size up the message bearers. Are they good at what they do? Are they trustworthy? Do you want to listen to them?

The knowledge required by today's workers, because of its highly tacit nature, will often be learned best in a group, coached, synchronous fashion. This does not mean that there is no place for self-paced learning. To address the explicit-knowledge aspects of these competencies (see example, below), self-paced, non-facilitated learning is effective. But in order to learn the judgment-laden "art" of being (say) a good manager, people will require some group-based, coached, synchonous, and face-to-face experiences. (Note that this does not necessarily mean traditional classroom experiences.)

USING THE MODEL

In the following example, an organization needs to help its sales force move from transactional to solution selling.

Example: The Learning Approaches Model

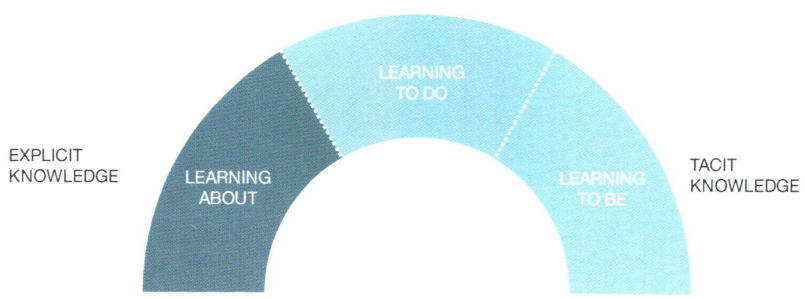

Issue: Moving from Transactional Selling to Solution Selling

Learning About:	Salespeople need to know more about available solutions, their customers' businesses, their own business, and industry trends.
Learning to Do:	Salespeople need to demonstrate specific skills and deliverables — such as asking better questions, concluding sales calls, developing account plans, and running team meetings.
Learning to Be:	Salespeople need to see themselves, their job, and their customers differently; to be guided by a consultative attitude that is "second nature" and helps them make good decisions in the moment.

Note the range of learning goals in this case: The organization's salespeople need to *know more about* certain things. They also need to be able to *demonstrate* specific skills and *produce* certain deliverables *better* than before. And, they need to *see* themselves and their customers *differently*.

In this example, a designer might create a learning system that included self-paced online courses and tools for the "learning about" goals; classroom sessions and virtual discussions for the "learning to do" goals; and personal coaching, manager-led reinforcement, and action learning projects for the "learning to be" goals.

It is not necessary to develop rigid recipes that match specific learning technologies with certain learning goals. What is important is for designers to:

- Ask the right questions in order to tease out the full range of learning goals implicit in a certain performance issue

- Be clear about which learning goals can realistically be met using a certain learning approach

The table on the next page presents a set of questions that designers can ask line managers or high performers in order to uncover a full range of learning goals inherent in an issue.

Questions to Uncover a Range of Learning Goals

Learning Goals	Questions to Ask
Learning about	What concepts or facts do people need to know?
	What rules, policies, or procedures must people be able to cite?
	On what things do we want people to be able to pass a written test?
	What "elevator speeches" should people be able to deliver?
Learning to do	What skills do we want people to be able to demonstrate?
	What deliverables must people be able to produce? With higher quality? With greater efficiency?
	What do we want to see people doing differently on the job (in discussions with employees, in the customer's office, in situation X)?
	When someone (an employee, a customer, a partner) says or does X, what would we like the person to say or do in response?
Learning to be	In what ways do people need to see the world (their customers, their employees, their organization) differently?
	What underlying principles or beliefs should be driving people's behaviors and attitudes?
	When people need to exercise judgment in tricky or "gray" situations, what bedrock attitudes and ideas should they be able to rely on?
	Which people should be models for the rest? What are they like? How do they act?

The Integrated Learning Model

- To provide a high-level framework for designing learning solutions

- To help sequence delivery methods effectively in a blended learning solution

The Integrated Learning Model

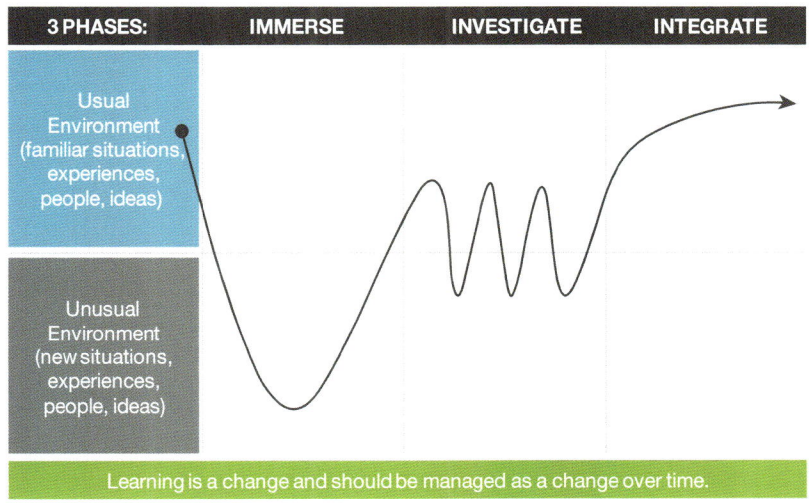

| 3 PHASES: | IMMERSE | INVESTIGATE | INTEGRATE |

Usual Environment (familiar situations, experiences, people, ideas)

Unusual Environment (new situations, experiences, people, ideas)

Learning is a change and should be managed as a change over time.

A WAVE OVER TIME

With today's broader range of learning delivery methods, combined with the move away from isolated learning events, it is helpful to have a framework for organizing a blended solution over time. Forum's Integrated Learning Model (see graphic above) moves learners between different environments and through different phases so that they develop new competencies.

Usual and Unusual Environments

To initiate the learning of leadership/customer competencies, it helps to move learners out of their usual environment—the places and situations that encourage settled habits and beliefs. Learning theorists such as Peter Senge and Jack Mezirow have written of the importance of "unfreezing" learners' mental models. Executive coaches talk about "holding a mirror" up to individuals, so they can see their behavior clearly. And, learners themselves talk about how the desire for learning or change is usually sparked by a disorienting or uncomfortable experience.

In addition to sparking new points of view, an unusual environment lends itself to more intriguing, compelling learning—or, as our interviewee David Carder puts it, "HCF: the High Cool Factor." The reality these days is that learners expect training to be both relevant *and* scintillating. Everyone is used to high-quality, all-pervasive media. Simply to grab people's attention, learning had better incorporate some HCF.

We believe that taking learners away from their everyday routine—providing a unique "space apart" where they can call their existing ideas into question and try on new ones—is an underestimated force for workplace learning and, moreover, one of the reasons why e-learning has often proved boring and disappointing when it is used alone. (Note that an unusual environment does not necessarily mean a *classroom* environment. The "space apart" could be a different job assignment, a web-based simulation, or a multi-player online scenario.)[16]

Three Learning Phases: Immerse, Investigate, and Integrate

Over time, the learner moves back and forth between the usual (or familiar) and the unusual (or unfamiliar) environments, passing through three phases of learning: 1) *Immerse*, in which the outcome is the unfreezing of mental models and the awareness that there is something new to consider; 2) *Investigate*, which is a time to try on, test, and practice new behaviors; and 3) *Integrate*, which results in the incorporation of new competencies into performance on the job. Each phase has distinct purposes, which relate back to the six Learning Principles:

- *Immerse:* To gain buy-in to the value of learning, to unfreeze learners' attitudes and beliefs, and to build the learning community

- *Investigate:* To provide an opportunity for reflective practice, to support and challenge learners as they experiment, and to involve learners in coaching and learning from one another

- *Integrate:* To embed new competencies in daily work, to solidify new behaviors and beliefs, and to extend the learning community

Purposes of Each Phase

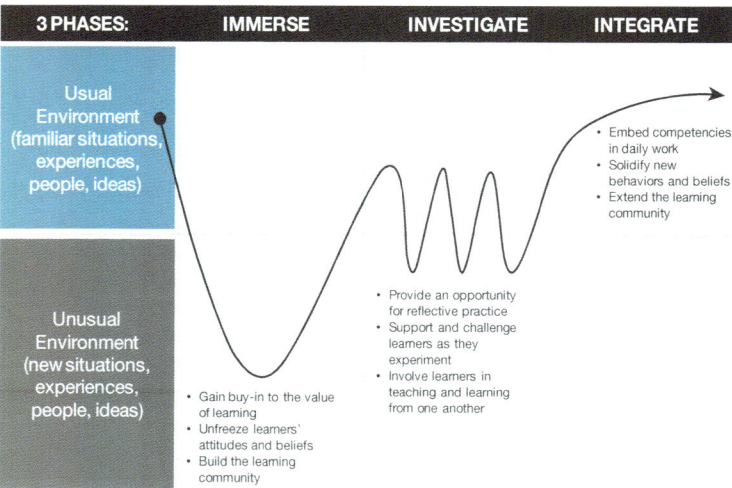

Sample Learning Objectives for Each Phase

Designers will be able to think of many possible learning objectives for each phase. Here are some examples:

Objectives for Immerse could be:

- Describe the value of doing A
- Express your positive and negative feelings about situation B
- Question the need for action C
- State several possible perspectives on situation D

Objectives for Investigate could be:

- Test procedure A in a protected setting
- Develop a plan with others to address situation B
- Describe your successes and mistakes with process C
- Request and provide coaching on skill D

Objectives for Integrate could be:

- Apply skill A regularly on the job
- Demonstrate behavior B in a customer situation
- Act as a model and coach for others on competency C
- Meet performance objective D

How Long Will It Take?

The three phases can unfold over a short or a long time—days, weeks, or months. The main point is that they represent a process, not an event. While it is true that learners can have breakthrough insights, it is unlikely that those insights will "stick" if there is no opportunity for investigation or integration. In addition, the process is often iterative. As learners move toward mastery of a complex set of competencies, they can benefit from returning several times to Immerse—for an energy boost, a course correction, or a new level of challenge.

Although almost any delivery method could be adapted to work for any phase of the model, certain methods lend themselves naturally to Immerse, Investigate, or Integrate. The graphic that follows shows the type of delivery methods that work best for each phase.

- In *Immerse,* delivery methods should facilitate buy-in and energy, new attitudes and frames of reference, and learning community. Ideally, they should take learners *away* from the everyday job.

- In *Investigate,* delivery methods should facilitate reflective practice, experimentation, and peer coaching and learning. Ideally, they should keep one *close* to the job.

- In *Integrate,* delivery methods should facilitate application to work, reinforcement of behaviors and beliefs, and extension of the learning community. Ideally, they should be a seamless *part* of the job.

Appropriate Delivery Methods

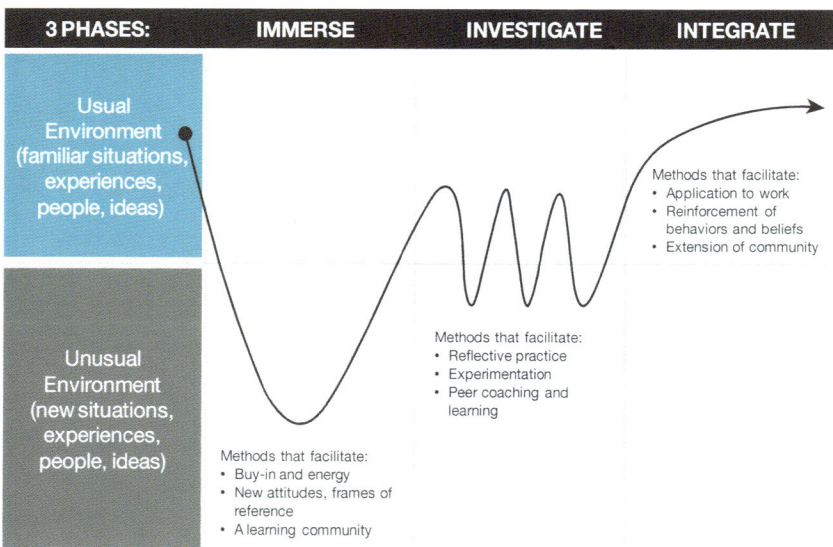

The next graphic shows how specific delivery methods match up with each of the phases. (These 12 delivery methods are ones that Forum utilizes in learning solutions.) We have found that it often works well to select one or two methods from each phase—for example, 1-2-2 or 1-2-1.

Delivery methods for Immerse include:

- On-the-job assignments
- Classroom sessions

- Virtual case discussion and scenarios

- Web-based simulations

Delivery methods for Investigate include:

- Team facilitation

- Web-based tutorials

- Action learning laboratories

- Virtual practice and role-play

- Personal coaching

Delivery methods for Integrate include:

- Manager-led reinforcement

- Virtual meetings

- Tool kits and job aids

12 Delivery Methods

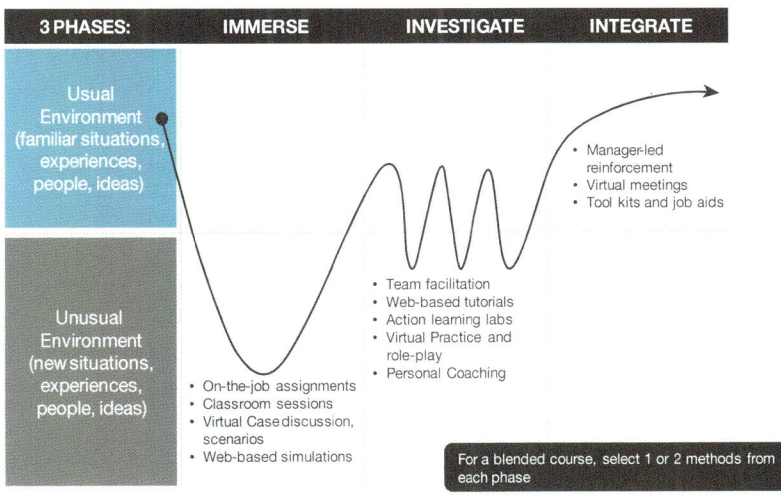

Tips for Designers

When putting together an integrated (blended) learning program, designers can apply the following tips:

- Sequence instructional strategies according to the three learning phases.

- Pick one or two appropriate delivery methods for each phase (often, a 1-2-2 pattern will work well: 1 for Immerse, 2 for Investigate, and 2 for Integrate).

- Include all three phases, even when the learning process is designed to be short.

- If there is time, consider an iterative process, where the learning cycles through the three phases two or more times.

And, keep the Learning Principles in mind. As Forum's Vivien Price puts it, "Blended learning fails when it is too complex, puts too much onus on the individual, provides no support, and is not relevant."

Immerse First?

How important is it to put Immerse, and its appropriate delivery methods, first? We, along with many other learning professionals, have in the past advocated a different sequence for blended learning, wherein participants first "learn the concepts" by doing extensive individual prework (paper- or web-based) and later come together for practice in a classroom setting. The theory is that this sequence makes the classroom learning more efficient, because people come in with the concepts already under their belt and are ready to practice. We have experimented with this design sequence and have found three difficulties when it is used to develop leadership or customer competencies:

1. The lack of an immersion experience (outside of their everyday routine) deprives learners of an opportunity to unfreeze their thinking, perceive a need for change, and see new possibilities—all critical success factors for leadership/customer learning.

2. It is extremely difficult to create motivation and enthusiasm for this type of learning using only brief telephone kickoff sessions or e-mails up front. Participants typically lack energy for the course until they meet face to face with one another and their facilitator.

3. Learners tend to perceive self-paced work as prework—in other words, something to be sidestepped if possible.

As a result, we recommend Immerse-Investigate-Integrate as a better sequence for leadership/customer learning. But, what happens if budget or time restrictions mean that learners and facilitators cannot physically come together? We offer two suggestions based on our research:

- *Be creative with the methods used for Immerse.* Instead of immersing participants in classroom learning, consider giving them a really unusual job assignment—perhaps one where they get to work with some new colleagues—and asking them to capture insights. Or, use online case studies and stories that draw a group together and provide an engaging basis for a series of asynchronous discussions. Sophisticated web-based simulations, if budget permits, can be another way to immerse learners in a "space apart." See Learning Principle 6, about designing learning communities, for more ideas on how to bring learners together mentally and emotionally, if not physically. The key is to generate plenty of energy and buy-in at the start.

- *Adjust goals toward "learning about"* (as opposed to "learning to be"). As the Learning Approaches Model indicates, people can easily acquire *explicit* knowledge without group-based learning. For example, salespeople can acquire knowledge about products, industry trends, their customers' businesses, and so on, in an individual self-paced fashion. *Tacit* knowledge, however, is much more difficult to acquire outside a social context. If time and budget allow only for bite-sized, individually based learning, one should recognize that the outcome will likely be "knowledge about" certain things—which may be a perfectly acceptable result.

LINK TO THE LEARNING APPROACHES MODEL

The following examples show how the Integrated Learning Model adapts to different learning goals. If the overall goal is "learning about," then delivery methods can be mostly individual, self-paced, and dispersed. If the overall goal is "learning to be," then the approach should include group, coached, synchronous, and face-to-face experiences.

Focus on "Learning About": Example

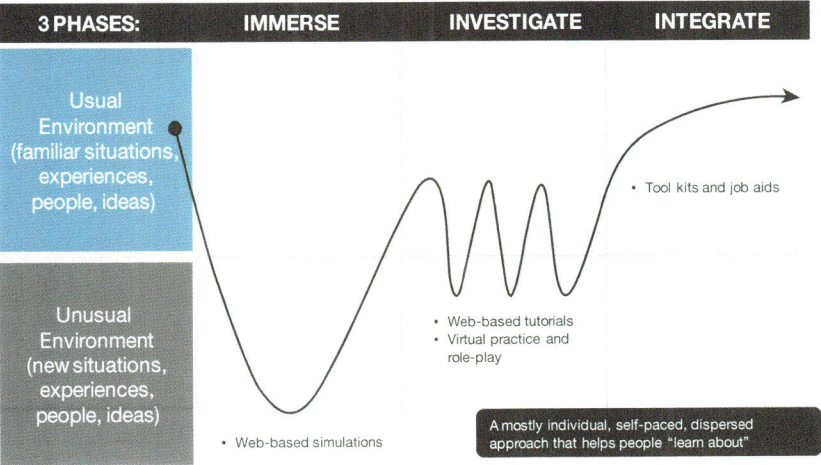

Focus on "Learning to Be": Example

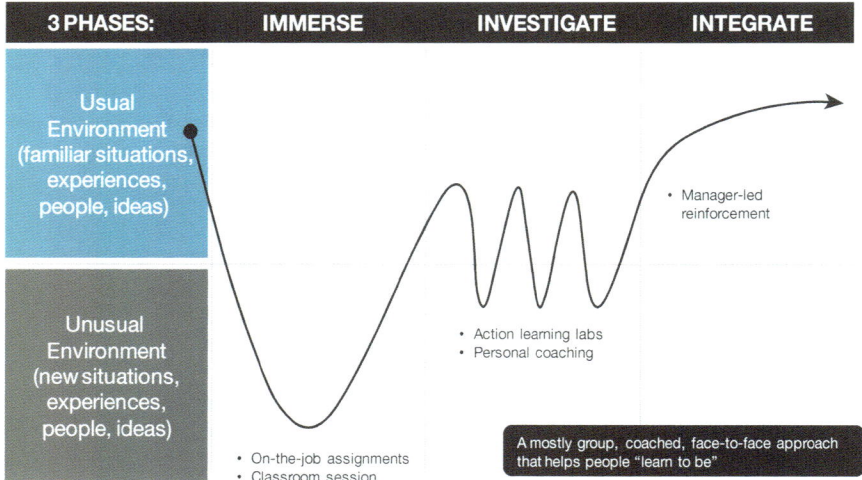

3 PHASES:	IMMERSE	INVESTIGATE	INTEGRATE

Usual Environment (familiar situations, experiences, people, ideas)

Unusual Environment (new situations, experiences, people, ideas)

- Manager-led reinforcement

- Action learning labs
- Personal coaching

- On-the-job assignments
- Classroom session

A mostly group, coached, face-to-face approach that helps people "learn to be"

Strategies for Learner Motivation

- To help designers and facilitators create effective strategies for motivating learners
- To help sequence those strategies appropriately

Strategies for Learner Motivation

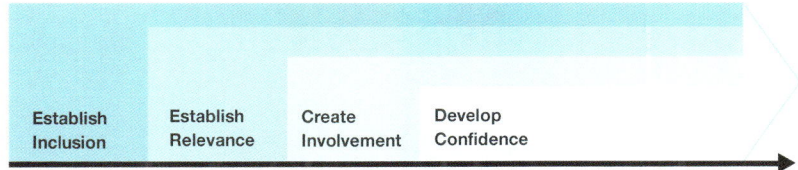

| Establish Inclusion | Establish Relevance | Create Involvement | Develop Confidence |

Course time

THE STRATEGIES

One of the things that characterize leadership/customer competencies is the complexity of the motivational issues surrounding them. While the Learning Approaches Model and the Integrated Learning Model help designers increase learner motivation by selecting the right learning methods and sequences, there are some more specific motivational strategies to be called out.

Learning expert Raymond J. Wlodkowski proposes a four-part motivational framework on which the following strategies are based:[18]

- *Establish inclusion:* Create an atmosphere in which learners feel recognized, respected, and connected.

- *Establish relevance:* Show how the learning is important to personal and organizational success.

- *Create involvement:* Draw on learners' knowledge and perspectives, and encourage them to drive their own learning.

- *Develop confidence:* Help learners see how they have become more competent and successful.

LINK TO THE INTEGRATED LEARNING MODEL

All four of these strategies will be useful at any point in a course or curriculum. There is a natural sequence to them, however, which links to the Integrated Learning Model:

- *Establish inclusion* and *establish relevance* are most critical during the Immerse phase.

- *Create involvement* is most critical during the Investigate phase.

- *Develop confidence* is most critical during the Integrate phase.

For example, a designer and/or facilitator concerned with the Immerse phase of a course should take extra care to be sure they are establishing inclusion and establishing relevance for the learners.

TACTICS

The table on the next page lists a set of 44 tactics that support the motivational strategies. To develop these tactics, we drew on Wlodkowski's work, Forum's Learning Principles, and our database of facilitation practices.

Motivational Strategies and Tactics

Strategies	Tactics
Establish Inclusion: Create an atmosphere in which learners feel respected, recognized, and connected	Allow for introductions
	Provide an opportunity for learners to share some information or stories about themselves
	Indicate your intention and willingness to help them learn
	Share something of value to you
	Introduce important norms and ground rules, and ask for learners' input
	When possible, reflect learners' language and perspectives
	Use collaborative learning activities
	Invite the expression of emotions about the learning, both positive and negative
	Acknowledge the importance of comfort zones and the difficulty of having our beliefs challenged
	Acknowledge the different ways of knowing, levels of skills, and perspectives within the group
Establish Relevance: Show how the learning is important to personal and organizational success	Clearly identify the learning objectives or goals of the course
	Emphasize the relationship of the topic to learners' lives and work
	Tie the learning to important organizational goals, strategies, or values
	Assess learners' previous experience with and attitudes toward the topic
	Ask learners what they already know about the topic and what they want to know about the topic
	Clearly give the purpose or rationale for activities and assignments
	Ensure that learners experience some success early in the course
	Ensure that early learning activities are engaging, novel, and stimulating
	Encourage learners to make choices that will affect the learning experience (for example, how, what, when, where, or with whom they learn)
	Use relevant models to demonstrate the learning you expect
	Use incentives, especially when learning activities are initially unappealing
	Help learners be aware of the natural consequences of their learning (or not learning)

Strategies	Tactics
Create Involvement: Draw on learners' knowledge and perspectives, and encourage them to drive their own learning	Minimize any strong negative emotions (such as fear, humiliation, and helplessness) surrounding the topic
	Help learners set personal goals for the course
	Use contracting methods to foster self-direction
	When appropriate, ask learners whether they can make a commitment to the learning task
	Provide effective feedback
	Help learners attribute their successes to their own knowledge and efforts
	Help learners see that they can overcome failures and mistakes through their own efforts
	Let learners know in advance how and when they will be expected to speak, present, or contribute
	Promote learner control over pace and timing
	Use a variety of teaching methods and activities to match different learning styles
	Give learners the responsibility to teach others
	Use self-assessment methods that encourage reflection and insight
Develop Confidence: Help learners see how they have become more competent and successful	Point out incremental improvements
	Clearly explain assessment tasks and criteria in advance
	Use real performance tasks to help learners see that they can apply their learning on the job
	Provide opportunities for learners to demonstrate their strengths
	Ensure that tests are fair, valid, and clear
	Offer praise and rewards for successful learning
	Communicate learners' successes to the group and to others who are important to them
	Acknowledge and affirm learners' contributions to the learning process
	Celebrate success and provide closure at the end of significant units of learning
	Provide ways for learners to keep in touch with each other after the formal learning has concluded

About the Authors

About the Authors

Elizabeth Griep is Vice President, Advanced Workplace Learning, at Forum. With over 20 years of experience in the workplace learning industry as a consultant, designer, facilitator, and global project leader, Elizabeth has worked with clients in a variety of industries including financial services, high technology, healthcare, insurance, automotive, aerospace, and utilities. As a pioneer of Networked Learning, Elizabeth is focused on the evolution of how learning happens in organizations today. Prior to joining Forum, Elizabeth spent 10 years in the financial services industry.

Jocelyn Davis is Executive Vice President, R&D, at Forum. Jocelyn is responsible for Forum's strategies regarding creating and leveraging intellectual property, which includes original research, learningware, consulting tools, and protocols, as well as other core content. Jocelyn is co-author of Forum's latest book, *Strategic Speed: Mobilize People, Accelerate Execution* (Harvard Business Press, 2010).

Simon Fowler is an R&D Associate, Advanced Workplace Learning, at Forum. Simon has a passion for new media technology and for workplace relationships and communities. He applies that to a pioneering approach to Forum's workplace learning research and product development as well as to Forum's internal working practices. Simon has a 20-year technology and training background in manufacturing, non-profit, finance and telecommunications, as well as extensive global cultural experience. Prior to joining Forum, Simon delivered training across the globe for Lucent Technologies.

Acknowledgments

Acknowledgments

We thank all those who contributed to this research, especially Robin Heyden and Neil Heyden whose expertise and insight on learning in higher education and in corporations has been invaluable. We thank also our clients for opening a window into their lives and experiences with great candor and humor.

THE CONTRIBUTORS

Tom Atkinson, Ph.D., is Director of Client Research at The Forum Corporation, where he has conducted research for over 25 years. As a researcher, he has conducted groundbreaking studies on such topics as how to increase sales and service effectiveness; how to prepare leaders to drive growth; how to enable companies to execute with speed; and how to create a high-performance organizational climate. Tom's findings, which have been published in the *Harvard Business Review,* are the foundation for many of Forum's learning programs.

Ed Boswell, Ph.D., is President and CEO of Forum. In addition to his duties as CEO, Ed advises senior executive teams involved in major organizational transformation initiatives. Prior to joining Forum in 1989, Ed led sales and service teams for IBM and served as an organizational consultant for Human Systems. Ed is co-author of Forum's latest book, *Strategic Speed: Mobilize People, Accelerate Execution.*

Aly Brandt is Executive Vice President, Global Sales, at Forum. Aly is global head of sales teams in the U.K., Middle East, Europe, Asia, and North America. With over 20 years of global business development experience, she is well networked in the global leadership development industry. Aly has served on multiple advisory boards, including a paid position as a Partner Development board member at Deloitte. For over 10 years, she has served as chairman of the board of Naked Angels, a nationally recognized original work theatre group based in New York City.

Christian Briggs is the founder of SociaLens, which promotes digital fluency in people and organizations. He is an Instructor of New Media Theory and a doctoral candidate in Human-Computer Interaction and Complex Systems at the Indiana University School of Informatics. He has worked in various creative, management, and consultative roles for Palladium Group, Ziff Davis Interactive, Surfwatch, Walt Disney Imagineering, One to One Interactive, and Walmart.

David Carder is Vice President, Executive Consultant, at Forum. David helps consultants and facilitator teams to design and execute strategy-driven development systems to accelerate revenue growth and increase customer satisfaction.

Ellen Foley is Executive Vice President, Client Engagement, at Forum. Ellen oversees the teams that deliver our client work around the world, including Engagement Management, Consulting & Design, Publications, and our Resource Network (ResNet). Ellen is a learning professional with nearly 30 years of experience. She has worked with clients in a variety of industries including financial services, high technology, healthcare, insurance, automotive, aerospace, and utilities. Before joining Forum, Ellen spent 10 years in the financial services industry as vice president and director of training and development for BayBanks, a regional bank in New England.

Judy Francolini is a Forum Associate, consultant, facilitator, executive coach, and trainer who focuses on principles of experiential learning, leadership development, and team effectiveness. Partnering with Fortune 500 executive leaders since 1985, she helps guide their organizations to achieve extraordinary business transformation results. Judy is the developer and co-facilitator of the Senior Executive Women's Leadership Program at Rutgers University, sponsored by the Institute of Women's Leadership and the Center for Women and Work at Rutgers University.

Robin Heyden is a freelance writer and education consultant, based in Boston, MA. She works with universities, national organizations, software developers, and publishers to develop online educational materials and experiences. Most recently her work has involved social media and virtual worlds, as they apply to teaching and learning.

Neil Heyden is an education marketing and strategy consultant living west of Boston, MA. He works with US and international K-16 and medical education institutions, multinational businesses, application developers, and educational publishers developing online and print learning and training materials and experiences. Recent collaborations include virtual world exploration, learning principles evaluation, and continuing medical education training.

Charles Jennings, Ph.D.,formerly Chief Learning Officer for Reuters and Thomson Reuters, is currently Managing Director of Duntroon Associates, a UK-based Learning, Performance, and Productivity consultancy company. He also leads a Workplace Learning research initiative of the European Foundation for Management Development (EFMD) In 2008 he was honored with the U.K. World of Learning "Outstanding Contribution to the Learning Industry" award in recognition of his work on performance improvement, and just-in-time and informal learning.

Ian Kristic, Ph.D., is Vice President, Executive Consultant, at Forum. Ian has held executive-level positions in consultancies such as Linkage and Executive Development Associates, where he designed and facilitated innovative leadership development experiences and talent management solutions for various organizations.

Molly McGinn, Ph.D., is a Forum Associate. A recipient of Forum's distinguished Chairman's Award, she is frequently called upon to add the "secret sauce" of creative spirit to instructional designs and push the envelope by developing creative learning experiences for global clients. Molly has taught and studied in Japan, at the University of Science and Technology in Sichuan Province in China and with the Academy of Science in Ulan Ude in Siberia. As the manager of United Airlines' training function in Asia, Molly served on the research team that branded United's business class service.

Dottie McKissick, Ph.D., is a Forum Associate and a highly experienced and innovative designer who has created many large-scale Forum learning systems in recent years in the areas of leadership (including leadership transition), sales, and sales management. A particular interest of hers is how to accelerate the onboarding of millennials and other early-career professionals into today's complex organizations. Her program—Work Positive! Strategies and Skills for Thriving in Your Organization—does just that by helping participants develop the artful, contextual skills of navigating their work space. Her publications include Pacific Rim, 2010, a strategic-planning scenario that identifies factors that will bear on capital investment decisions throughout the Pacific Rim in the 21st century and Performance-Based Leadership

Michele McMahon is Senior Vice-President, Delivery, at Forum. Michele heads up a team of program managers in EMEA who lead enterprisewide learning initiatives. She also serves as an executive consultant on Forum client teams. A 20-year veteran of Forum, Michele has worked with senior client leaders on numerous global projects in a variety of industries: energy, financial services, technology, manufacturing, and consumer products.

Srini S. Pillay, M.D., is the CEO of NeuroBusiness Group, an executive coaching company focused on enhancing social intelligence in companies. Srini is an internationally recognized executive coach, public speaker, psychiatrist, and brain imaging researcher who is focused on the fields of personal and organizational transformation. As a "certified master coach," Srini was on the faculty of the Behavioral Coaching Institute where he taught international business executives from a variety of different companies, including Fortune 500 companies, the art of coaching, with a special emphasis on using neuroscience to enhance communication, decision making, and transformation.

Vivien Price is Vice President, Instructional Design, at Forum. Viv heads the Instructional Design team at Forum. She specializes in teamwork and leadership, sales, negotiation, and key account management learning systems. Viv joined Forum Europe in 1996 and moved to the U.S. in 2000.

David Robertson is Vice President, Executive Consultant, at Forum. David provides business-development support and senior-level design, development, and piloting of learning solutions in sales, service, leadership, and customer experience. David's 30+ years experience in the training industry has included spells at IBM, National Semiconductor (U.K.) Ltd., British Aerospace, and Grand Metropolitan.

George Siemens is affiliated with the Technology Enhanced Knowledge Research Institute (TEKRI) at Athabasca University. His role as a social media strategist involves planning, researching, and implementing social networked technologies, with focus on systemic impact and institutional change. He is the author of *Knowing Knowledge* (2006) and the *Handbook of Emerging Technologies for Learning* (2009).

Client Contributors

Eden Alvarez-Backus, Chief Learning Officer, National Grid

Chrissy Amure-Butcher, Director, Global Leadership Development, American Express

Ed Flahive, Chief Talent Officer, State Street Bank

Jeffrey Hickman, Learning & Development Program Manager, ARAMARK

Kate Hoepfner-Karle, Director, Global Leadership & Development, Covidien

Rick Lyman, Vice President, Global HR Operations, Cisco

Lisa Miller, Director, Learning and Organizational Development Systems—Global, Carlson Wagonlit Travel

Seth Moeller, Director, Leadership Development

Chris Newman, Vice President, Learning & Organizational Development, Boston Financial

Kirstin Normandin, Director, Global Leadership & Development, Covidien

Dr. Shirli Pollard, CPT, Learning and Knowledge Management Performance Lead, Air Products and Chemicals, Inc.

Jonathan Rosin, Vice President Leadership & Development

Tiffany Sellers, Director of On-Board & Branding, ARAMARK

Suchan Sivam, Vice President, Talent Management, State Street Bank

Jennifer Tice, Vice President, Management and Professional Development

Dale Wallace, Learning & Development, ARAMARK

Kit Williams, Director, Learning & Organizational Development, Genzyme

Bibliography

Bibliography

Andresen, Bent, "Scenario Planning and Learning Technologies: The Foundation of Lifelong Learning," *IFIP International Federation for Information Processing,* vol. 281, pp. 29-36, 2008.

Annual Survey Report 2010 on Learning & Talent and Development, Chartered Institute of Personnel and Development.

Army Excellence in Leadership (AXL), "A Multimedia Approach to Building Tacit Knowledge and Cultural Reasoning," U.S. Army Research Institute; USC Institute for Creative Technologies; Kansas State University Consortium Research Fellows Program.

Bersin, Josh, "The High-Impact Learning Organization," Bersin & Associates, 2008.

Boud, David, Peter Cressey, and Peter Docherty, *Productive Reflection at Work: Learning for Changing Organizations* (London: Routledge, 2006).

Brogan, Chris, and Julien Smith, *Trust Agents* (New York: Wiley, 2009).

Brown, John Seely, and Richard P. Adler, "Minds on Fire: Open Education, the Long Tail, and Learning," *Educause Review,* vol. 43, no. 1, January/February 2008.

Casebow, Peter, and Owen Ferguson, "The Learning and Performance Link—How Managers Learn (In Their Own Words)," *GoodPractice* http://*www.improvementnetwork.gov.uk/imp/aio/1119018* (Accessed June 1st 2010).

Conner, Marcia L., and James G. Clawson. *Creating a Learning Culture: Strategy, Technology, and Practice* (Cambridge, England: Cambridge University Press, 2004).

Cross, Jay, *Informal Learning: Rediscovering the Natural Pathways That Inspire Innovation and Performance* (San Francisco: Pfeiffer/Wiley, 2007).

Cross, Jay, and the Internet Time Alliance, *Working Smarter,* Internet Time Group 2010.

Darling, Marilyn, Charles Parry, and Joseph Moore, "Learning in the Thick of It," *Harvard Business Review*, July 2005.

Dede, Chris, "Planning for Neomillennial Learning Styles," *Educause Quarterly,* vol. 28, no. 1, Accessed June 1, 2010.

Edmondson, Amy C, "The Competitive Imperative of Learning," *Harvard Business Review,* July 2008.

Erickson, Tamara J., "The Leaders We Need Now," *Harvard Business Review,* May 2010.

Goldsmith, Marshall, Howard J. Morgan, and Alexander J. Ogg, *Leading Organizational Learning: Harnessing the Power of Knowledge* (San Francisco: Jossey-Bass, 2004).

Halpern, D., "Applying the Science of Learning: Using the Principles of Cognitive Psychology to Enhance Teaching and Learning," *http://www.au.af.mil/au/awc/awcgate/congress/halpern.htm* Retrieved July 9 2010.

Heifetz, Ronald, Marty Linsky, and Alexander Grashow, *The Practice of Adaptive Leadership* (Cambridge: Harvard Business Press, 2009).

Heifetz, Ronald, and Marty Linsky, *http://www.hks.harvard.edu/news-events/news/commentary/making-decisions-outside-repertoire* Retrieved July 8 2010.

Heiphetz, Alex, and Gary Woodill, *Training and Collaboration with Virtual Worlds: How to Create Cost-saving, Efficient, and Engaging Programs* (New York: McGraw-Hill, 2010).

Jafferty, Jubal, Agilent Technologies, "Learning as Part of Work, Not Apart from Work," Presentation at Bersin Associates Impact 2010 Conference.

Kolb, David, *Experiential Learning: Experience as the Source of Learning and Development* (Englewood Cliffs, NJ: Prentice-Hall, 1983).

McAfee, Andrew, *Enterprise 2.0: New Collaborative Tools for Your Organization's Toughest Challenges* (Boston: Harvard Business, 2009).

Marsick, Victoria J. and Karen E. Watkins, *The New Update on Adult Learning Theory,* chap. 3, "Informal and Incidental Learning," (San Francisco: Jossey-Bass, 2001), *http://www.fsu.edu/~elps/ae/download/ade5385/Marsick.pdf*

Maznevski, M.L., and K.M. Chudoba, "Bridging Space over Time: Global Virtual-Team Dynamics and Effectiveness," *Organization Science,* vol. 11, pp. 473-492, 2000.

Metiri Group, "Multimodal Learning Through Media: What the Research Says," Commissioned by Cisco.

Perkins, D., "Teaching for Understanding," *American Educator,* vol. 17, no. 3, pp. 8, 28-35, Fall 1993, *http://www.exploratorium.edu/IFI/resources/workshops/teachingforunderstanding.html Retrieved July 8 2010.*

Pfeffer, Jeffrey, and Robert Sutton, "The Knowing-Doing Gap: How Smart Companies Turn Knowledge into Action" (Cambridge: Harvard Business School Press, 1999), *http://www.providersedge.com/docs/book_reviews/Knowing-Doing_Gap.pdf*

Pink, Daniel H., *Drive: The Surprising Truth about What Motivates Us* (New York: Riverhead, 2009).

Rock, David, *Your Brain at Work: Strategies for Overcoming Distraction, Regaining Focus, and Working Smarter All Day Long* (New York: Harper Business, 2009).

Schank, Roger C., *Lessons in Learning, E-learning, and Training: Perspectives and Guidance for the Enlightened Trainer* (San Francisco: Pfeiffer, 2005).

Schrage, Michael. Serious Play: How the World's Best Companies Simulate to Innovate. Boston, Mass.: Harvard Business School, 2000. Print.

Siemens, George, *Knowing Knowledge,* Creative Commons, *www.knowingknowledge.com*, 2006.

Smith, M. K. (2003, 2009) "Communities of practice," the encyclopedia of informal education, *www.infed.org/biblio/communities_of_practice.htm. Retrieved June 23 2010*

Talbot, J., "Workers Researching the Workplace Using a Work-based Learning Framework: Towards an Agenda for Improving Supervisory Practice," *Impact: Journal of Applied Research in Workplace E-learning,* vol. 1, no. 1, pp. 169–182, 2009.

Tapscott, Don, *Grown up Digital: How the Net Generation Is Changing Your World* (New York: McGraw-Hill, 2009).

Thalheimer, Will, "Aligning the Learning and Performance Contexts: Creating Spontaneous Remembering," © 2002-2009 *http://www.work-learning.com/catalog*

Endnotes

Endnotes

1 R. Van Lee, L. Fabish, and N. McGraw, "The Value of Corporate Values," Strategy + Business, issue 39, Spring 2005; "Business 2010: Embracing the Challenge of Change," *Economist Intelligence Unit,* 2005; and "Building a Nimble Organization, A McKinsey Global Survey," 2006.

2 "High-Impact Learning Practices: An Operating Guide for the Modern Corporate Learning Function," v. 1.0, © Bersin and Associates Industry Study, David Mallon, Senior Analyst, July 2009.

3 Chris Dede, "Planning for 'Neomillennial' Learning Styles: Implications for Investments in Technology and Faculty," Harvard Graduate School of Education, August 2004.

4 Lowell Bryan and Claudia Joyce, "The 21st Century Organization," *The McKinsey Quarterly,* no. 3, 2005, pp. 24-33.

5 Scott C. Beardsley, Bradford C. Johnson, and James Manyika, "Competitive Advantage from Better Interactions," *The McKinsey Quarterly,* no. 2, 2006, p. 55.

6 Marilyn Darling, Charles Parry and Joseph Moore, "Learning in the Thick of It," *Harvard Business Review,* July 2005.

7 Quoted in Pfeffer, Jeffrey, and Robert Sutton, *The Knowing-Doing Gap: How Smart Companies Turn Knowledge into Action* (Cambridge: Harvard Business School Press, 1999), *http://www.providersedge.com/docs/book_ reviews/Knowing-Doing_Gap.pdf*

8 David Rock, *Your Brain at Work: Strategies for Overcoming Distraction, Regaining Focus, and Working Smarter All Day Long* (New York: Harper Business, 2009).

9 Amy Edmondson, "The Competitive Imperative of Learning," *Harvard Business Review,* July 2008.

10 Richard J. Light, *Making the Most of College: Students Speak Their Minds* (Cambridge: Harvard University Press, 2001). For a summary of Light's research, see Richard Light, "The College Experience: A Blueprint for Success," *http://athome.harvard.edu/programs/light/index.html*

11 John Seely Brown and Paul Duguid, "Organizational Learning and Communities of Practice," *Organization Science,* vol. 2, no. 1, pp. 40-57, 1991; A. Ardichvili, V. Page, and T. Wentling, T., "Motivation and barriers to participation in virtual knowledge sharing teams," *Journal of Knowledge Management,* vol. 7, no. 1, pp. 64-77, 2003.

12 www.dennisonculture.com

13 A formal, detailed learning environment assessment is available from Forum. The assessment diagnoses current actions within the organization that support learning on the job. The results of the assessment help define the primary- and secondary-level ownership of sustainment activities.

14   Thomas H. Davenport and Laurence Prusack, *Working Knowledge: How Organizations Manage What They Know* (Cambridge: Harvard Business Press, 2000), page 71.

15   Forum designers and some Forum clients are familiar with a previous "flexible learning technologies" model, similar to this one, which suggested appropriate approaches to "learning of the heart, learning of the hands, and learning of the head." Envisioned as a series of nested boxes, these learning domains were defined according to the degree of emotion, skill, or knowledge involved. Although this model was a useful tool, our interviewees cited several issues with it:

- A high degree of emotion around an issue is not the only reason for bringing people together to learn; for example, "head work" concerning strategy can be complex enough to warrant group sessions.

- In any learning situation, we should be engaging the learner's emotions, skills, *and* intellect. Because they are so intertwined, "heart, hands, head" may not help us in parsing out different learning goals and the best corresponding approaches.

- The model could be presented in a simpler manner (for example, we don't really need two dimensions).

"Heart, hands, head" and "tacit-explicit" are different ways to think about learning goals. We believe the tacit-explicit continuum is a little more helpful and accurate. One might possibly draw a correspondence between *heart* and learning to be, *hands* and learning to do, and *head* and learning about; in the Learning Approaches model, however, emotion vs. intellect is not the basis for distinctions among learning approaches.

16   Fans of Joseph Campbell may be interested to know that there are similarities between this model and Campbell's "Hero's Journey" story archetype, described in his book *The Hero with a Thousand Faces.* As Chris Vogler notes in *The Writer's Journey* (his take on Campbell's ideas): "For the writer, producer, or designer, (Campbell's) concepts are a welcome tool kit, stocked with sturdy instruments ideal for the craft of storytelling. With these tools you can construct a story … that will be dramatic, entertaining, and psychologically true." In our work with clients, we have found the Hero's Journey Model to be extremely useful not only as a storytelling framework but also as an instructional design framework or device—which is not surprising, since drama, entertainment, and psychological truth are virtues for learning as well as for storytelling. Those who wish to see the similarities between the Integrated Learning Model and the Hero's Journey can read pages 9 to 27 of *The Writer's Journey, 3ʳᵈ Edition,* by Chris Vogler (Studio City, CA: Michael Wiese Productions, 2007).

17 Forum designers and some of our clients are familiar with a previous
Forum learning model that laid out three learning phases (Preparation,
Apprenticeship, Mastery) and three types of activities

(Awareness, Practice, Application). The Integrated Learning Model
essentially brings those two dimensions together in a framework
that is simpler and more broadly applicable today. The Preparation-
Apprenticeship-Mastery framework is most appropriate when one is
trying to develop individuals' expertise over the long term. The I-I-I
model applies easily to a broader range of learning situations and offers
more specific guidance to learning designers.

18 Raymond J. Wlodkowski, et al., *Adult Learning: Theories, Principles, and
Applications* (Phoenix, AZ: University of Phoenix, 2001).

17231242R20058

Made in the USA
Charleston, SC
02 February 2013